"Dr. Kent Brantly is responsible for one of the worst weeks of my life. When I told him that, he smiled and said, 'It wasn't that great for me either!' But Kent gives God the credit for saving his life and surviving the deadly Ebola virus that infected him while serving others in the name of Jesus. Dr. Brantly and his wife, Amber, went obediently to Liberia to serve with Samaritan's Purse as medical missionaries, and were the recipients of prayers from around the world as they battled an attack that threatened their future. The world watched as Kent was successfully transported back to the United States from Africa. International media outlets captured his every step as he walked from the ambulance into Atlanta's Emory University Hospital, where he found physical restoration—a miracle from God. You will be riveted by this extraordinary couple who are called for life to serve the Lord Jesus Christ—the Great Physician!"

—Franklin Graham, president and CEO, Samaritan's Purse
and Billy Graham Evangelistic Association

"When hope seems dim, *Called for Life* reminds us of the limitless possibilities of a God-driven life. Dr. Brantly's story inspires us to stay strong in the unexpected crises of life . . . to be encouraged to recall God's promises . . . to be challenged to examine our own commitment to God's call on our lives."

—Max Lucado, pastor and best-selling author

"Compelling, factual, and emotional, *Called for Life* draws readers to reflect on their own journeys to faith in Christ and encourages them to trust God in the crises of life."

—Nancy Writebol, SIM missionary to Liberia and fellow
Ebola survivor

"*Called for Life* invites all of us behind the curtain of the news stories and press releases and into the Brantlys' lives during the most trying of times. Their love for each other, their faith and courage, as well as the strength and support they received from their network of friends, family, and caregivers is heartwarming and inspiring. When we set out to just do what is right, this behind-the-news-flash story reminds all of us that we live in a global community, that we all have a role to play, and that all of us can make a difference, wherever we are and in whatever profession."

—LISA HENSLEY, virologist and deputy director at the National
Institute of Allergy and Infectious Disease, Integrated Research
Facility

"As you walk alongside them on their journey, Kent and Amber's poignant story will touch your heart, move you to tears, strengthen your faith, and cause you to trust God more."

—DAVID STEVENS, MD, MA (Ethics), CEO of the Christian
Medical and Dental Associations

"Kent and his wife, Amber, have truly lived by the phrase 'When the going gets tough, the tough go back to their calling.' Their great compassion for the sick and broken—choosing to suffer alongside them even in the face of possible death—has touched and saved many lives. I am thrilled to see the Brantlys share their amazing story in print, and I know it will inspire and challenge you to find your place in God's calling upon your life."

—DR. RAVI ZACHARIAS, author and speaker

"*Called for Life* tells the rest of the story—what went before, lay behind, and follows after the iconic images of a coverall-clad figure gently stepping out of an ambulance and into an international spotlight. Kent and Amber have given us a glimpse inside their previously private world to uncover the roots of their genuine humility, tender love for each other, and deep compassion for their neighbors. Not all readers will fully resonate with their interpretations, but all will surely appreciate their candor, sensitivity, and sincerity . . . and the beauty and suspense of a story well told."

—DAVID McRAY, MD, professor at the University
of Tennessee College of Medicine

"There are many books about surviving illness, but this is a one-of-a-kind story. What happens when ordinary Christian medical missionaries are caught up in an extraordinary world crisis? Though I know the story, I found my heart pounding as I turned the pages. And it turns out to be a tale not of disease, primarily, but of calling, faith, and love. It is a story of a remarkable family, their community, and their commitment to a hurting world and to God."

    —RANDY HARRIS, spiritual director and instructor,
       Abilene Christian University

"Knowing Kent and Amber personally, I can say that *Called for Life* is a deep and honest testament to God's working in the midst of suffering and crisis. Kent and Amber's voices come through the pages in a very authentic way, and you will experience all Kent's emotions as he walks through this journey. As an Ebola survivor myself, I wholeheartedly recommend this book."

    —RICK SACRA, MD, SIM missionary

"Refreshingly, the Brantlys never give trite answers to complex questions like 'How does God work in healing?' or 'Why is there suffering in the world?' Instead, what they give us is a story—their story, and it's one worth reading."

    —JONATHAN STORMENT, preaching minister at the Highland Church
       of Christ and co-author of *Bringing Heaven to Earth*

Called *for* Life

Called *for* Life

How Loving Our Neighbor
Led Us into the Heart of
the Ebola Epidemic

Kent & Amber
BRANTLY

with David Thomas

WATERBROOK
PRESS

CALLED FOR LIFE
Published by WaterBrook Press
12265 Oracle Boulevard, Suite 200
Colorado Springs, Colorado 80921

This book is not intended to replace the medical advice of a trained medical professional. Readers are advised to consult a physician or other qualified health-care professional regarding treatment of their medical problems. The author and publisher specifically disclaim liability, loss, or risk, personal or otherwise, which is incurred as a consequence, directly or indirectly, of the use or application of any of the contents of this book.

All Scripture quotations, unless otherwise indicated, are taken from the Holy Bible, New International Version®, NIV®. Copyright © 1973, 1978, 1984 by Biblica Inc.™ Used by permission of Zondervan. All rights reserved worldwide. www.zondervan.com. The Scripture quotation on page 140 is taken from the NIV 2011 edition. Scripture quotations marked (NLT) are taken from the Holy Bible, New Living Translation, copyright © 1996, 2004, 2007, 2013. Used by permission of Tyndale House Publishers Inc., Carol Stream, Illinois 60188. All rights reserved.

Italics in Scripture quotations reflect the authors' added emphasis.

Names and details in some anecdotes and stories have been changed to protect the identities of the persons involved.

Hardcover ISBN 978-1-60142-823-3
eBook ISBN 978-1-60142-824-0

Jacket design by Mark D. Ford; author photos by Gaylon Wampler; ambulance photo by AP Photo / WSB-TV Atlanta

Published in the United States by WaterBrook Multnomah, an imprint of the Crown Publishing Group, a division of Penguin Random House LLC, New York.

WATERBROOK and its deer colophon are registered trademarks of Penguin Random House LLC.

The Cataloging-in-Publication Data is on file with the Library of Congress.

Printed in the United States of America
2015—First Edition

10 9 8 7 6 5 4 3 2 1

SPECIAL SALES
Most WaterBrook Multnomah books are available at special quantity discounts when purchased in bulk by corporations, organizations, and special-interest groups. Custom imprinting or excerpting can also be done to fit special needs. For information, please e-mail SpecialMarkets@WaterBrookMultnomah.com or call 1-800-603-7051.

This book is dedicated to Bobby, James, and the more than 11,000 other people who lost their lives in the Ebola epidemic of 2013–15.

∽

May your suffering and your families' losses not be in vain.

Contents

PART 5: RESCUED!

PART 6: NEXT STEPS

GUINEA, SIERRA LEONE, AND LIBERIA

AFRICA

GUINEA

CONAKRY

SIERRA LEONE

GUECKEDOU

KAILAHUN • FOYA

KENEMA

FREETOWN

LIBERIA

GBARNGA

MONROVIA

NEW KRU TOWN

DUALA MARKET

WEST POINT

JACOB TOWN

MONROVIA

JFK MEDICAL CENTER

TO HARBEL/FIRESTONE/ROBERTS INTERNATIONAL AIRPORT

ELWA HOSPITAL

So What's Next?

K ent, bud. We got your test result. And I'm really sorry to tell you that it is positive for Ebola."

I had not expected to hear those words despite the mounting evidence over the past three days—the worsening symptoms, the repeated negative malaria tests—that would have led me to suspect Ebola had I been the doctor rather than the patient.

Our first Ebola patient had come to our hospital in Monrovia, Liberia, barely six weeks earlier. But we had worked under the strain of a looming Ebola outbreak for nearly three anxious months before then. For the thirty-eight years since Ebola Virus Disease had been identified, every outbreak had been limited to small rural communities.

This time, however, was different. This time, Ebola had found the perfect storm of factors, quickly spreading through three countries and into major urban centers.

Our hospital of forty-five to fifty beds hurriedly converted the chapel into a small isolation unit, hoping it would never be needed. When our first Ebola patient arrived, we maintained the only treatment unit in all of southern Liberia.

In the beginning stages of what erupted into the worst Ebola outbreak the world has ever seen, I had learned to consider Ebola anytime a patient entered our emergency room with a fever and symptoms that, just a few months earlier, would have been suspected as likely malaria or typhoid fever. In fact, for the safety of our medical workers, we treated all febrile patients as though they had Ebola until proven otherwise. It was too risky not to.

The Ebola strain we observed carried a mortality rate of 70 percent. The death rate was even higher in our hospital, where only one of the dozens of patients who had tested positive for Ebola had survived.

One.

Ebola didn't just kill our patients; it stripped them of their dignity. Ebola humiliated its victims by taking away control of their bodily functions. We constantly changed diapers and sheets and cleaned up patients, and we fed them when they could no longer do so themselves.

Unable to cure their disease, we focused on treating their sense of isolation that came from being in a treatment unit where only two groups of people were allowed inside. One group was the medical personnel always working with their own safety in the front of their minds in light of the disproportionate number of health-care workers contracting the disease. The second group was other Ebola patients, moaning and groaning in pain until their bodies could fight no longer.

For all but that one patient, a positive Ebola test had become a death sentence served out among suffering patients and cautious medical personnel—some unknown foreigners, even—outfitted so securely that only our eyes were visible through the protective goggles.

No families. No friends. No familiar faces. No human contact.

With no cure, no hope.

As the outbreak had worsened and our hospital worked to expand our capacity, I was named director of the treatment unit. I became the physician who ensured that our staff was properly trained, repeatedly reassuring them that when we followed the protocols and worked together as a team, we were completely safe. The staff had trusted me too, because for each of my patients, I had determined to display compassion over fear.

And now Dr. Lance Plyler, the team leader responsible for managing our medical response to Ebola, was standing outside my bedroom window, because he could not come into my contaminated home, notifying me that I, too, had contracted the virus. Dr. John Fankhauser, my colleague and mentor in Liberia for nine busy months, stood beside my bed dressed in full personal protective equipment (PPE), just as I had stood beside the beds of too many patients in our Ebola unit, because he wanted to be with me when Lance delivered the news.

"I really wish you hadn't said that," I told Lance.

I was so sick at that point that I don't remember saying those words; that is Lance's recollection of my reaction. But I do remember what I said immediately after.

"Okay, so what is next? What's our plan? What are we going to do?"

I am a doctor, trained to respond to a bad test result by creating a plan. More importantly, I am a husband and a father, and my thoughts turned to my beautiful wife and children back home in the United States. I might not see them, much less touch them, ever again.

I stared out our bedroom window, looking to Lance.

"How am I going to tell Amber?"

PART I

CRISIS

Defenseless

Kent

This is it. Everything is about to change.

Our first Ebola patient looked up at me weakly as I knelt next to her bed of blankets on the patio near the hospital pharmacy. The disease we had prepared for while praying we would never see it had, indeed, arrived at our hospital, and I realized I was about to set the tone for the rest of our time treating Ebola patients—however long that might prove to be.

Dressed in full protective gear, I offered the young woman my right hand protected by two surgical gloves. She grabbed hold.

"Felicia, my name is Dr. Brantly," I said. "This is David. He's one of our nurses."

David greeted her.

"We are going to take good care of you here," I assured Felicia.

It was Wednesday night, June 11, 2014. Our hospital had the only Ebola treatment unit in Liberia's capital city of Monrovia, and the phone call had come earlier in the evening from the country's Ministry of Health. Two suspected Ebola patients were being transferred to us from a hospital in the northern suburb of New Kru Town.

Three members of a family had died in the past week, and Ebola was the suspected cause. Two other family members had become sick and were at that hospital. As we began preparing our Ebola treatment unit, which had been sitting empty for months, we did not know when to expect the two.

We were not even sure they would actually come to us.

Nancy Writebol came in to help. Nancy, personnel director for Serving In Mission (SIM) missionaries in Liberia, had volunteered to serve as the unit's hygienist when we ramped up our Ebola response. Nancy changed the sheets on the beds and mixed a sufficient quantity of the bleach-water solution for decontamination.

Dr. Debbie Eisenhut (known as Dr. Debbie) volunteered to stay at the hospital and said she would call me at home if anything developed. A little later, Debbie did call, telling me an ambulance had arrived at the hospital with two patients, a man in his midforties and his niece. I returned to the hospital.

As our two patients waited outside in the ambulance, we had to recruit two staff members willing to be the first to risk their lives to work in the unit with our first Ebola patients. I did not expect anyone to *want* to sign up.

I pleaded with some of the nurses: "Look, this is somebody's sister, somebody's mother, somebody's daughter. Somebody's uncle, somebody's brother, somebody's cousin. We've got to take care of them. Think if this was your family member."

Our medical director at ELWA, Dr. Jerry Brown, joined in recruiting nurses by phone.

Two volunteered for the job: Louise, an ER nurse, and David, a nurse's aide.

Preparing the unit, assembling the staff, and getting the four of us dressed in PPE required a couple of hours. Debbie made several trips outside to the ambulance during that span. Each time Debbie went outside, she told everyone to remain near the ambulance and not to get out to walk around or enter the hospital until we came to get them.

There were no ambulance services in Monrovia. The only ambulances were owned by hospitals and the government for transporting patients from one hospital to another. An ambulance was typically a modified Land Cruiser with sideways-facing seats in the back. The crew sat in the front seat with no divider between them and the patient or patients in the back.

The ambulance outside our hospital contained three crew members, the two patients, and two family members—a man in his thirties and a boy who appeared to be twelve.

As we were preparing the unit, the uncle, who had been alert and talking, became very still and silent. The two family members helped Felicia climb down out of the ambulance and lie on the asphalt road behind it.

One of Felicia's relatives then grew angry at having to wait and stormed the entrance to the emergency room, kicking a hole in the door. He accused us of delaying care for Felicia and not being willing to admit her.

We tried to convince the family that we were not ignoring them, that we were preparing the best we could to take care of Felicia the right way and safely. He calmed down and returned to the ambulance.

Then it began raining. I do not know if Felicia walked or if she was carried, but they moved her to a covered porch in front of the hospital pharmacy and spread blankets there for her to lie on.

After we had the inside of the unit fully prepared, David and I suited up in PPE and approached Felicia on the porch. As I dropped to one knee beside her, the burden of the moment descended squarely on my shoulders, because I had known all along that once the first case arrived, working and living in Monrovia would never be the same.

"We have a stretcher," I told Felicia, "and we are going to put you on the stretcher and carry you to a place we have prepared for you."

I looked up at David. "Do you want her head or feet?"

"Feet," he replied.

I picked Felicia up by the shoulders, and we slid her onto the stretcher and placed the blankets on top of her. We carried her around the back of the hospital and into the isolation unit.

Dr. Debbie and Louise were waiting for her inside. I picked up a spray can of the chlorine solution and walked back around the hospital to the ambulance. Felicia's uncle remained curled up inside the ambulance, lying over the top of a backpack. I leaned into the truck and felt for a pulse, then looked him over. He was obviously deceased.

"I have to have that backpack," the man with him said. "It has my identification card in it."

I pulled the backpack out from under the uncle. The body fell onto the floor of the ambulance, his position unchanged. He still looked as though he were lying over the backpack. Rigor mortis had already set in.

I stood there, backpack in hand, facing a decision.

I could not give a backpack contaminated with Ebola to the man. But on the other hand, he had already been exposed, having ridden in the back of the ambulance and having taken care of the uncle and Felicia. I handed him the backpack.

The young boy started crying.

"Stop crying!" the man scolded him.

"It's okay for him to cry," I said. "You may be used to being around death, but he is twelve years old. He has lost four family members in a week. It's okay for him to be scared and to cry."

I sprayed bleach on the back of the ambulance and the road and porch where Felicia had been lying. I sprayed the door of the ER that had been kicked in and everything along the paths in between.

The leader of the ambulance team and I agreed that they would return the body to Redemption Hospital and we would take care of Felicia. None of the three crew members were wearing PPE. Not even a single pair of rubber gloves.

The man and the boy said they would ride in the ambulance back to Redemption. I didn't like that idea.

"It's fine," the man said. "It's just a dead body."

It was not just a dead body; it was a body loaded with a deadly virus.

❧

The health-care system in Liberia was not prepared for Ebola.

During Felicia's first two days with us, her mental state waxed and waned. She would sit up and talk with the nurses and we would feed her, then she would lie down and become unresponsive for an hour. Then she would sit back up and want to eat or talk.

On the third day, Felicia's condition improved. She was awake and alert more than she was out of it. Her fever came down. We hoped that she had turned a corner and would make it, that our first Ebola patient would survive.

The next day, June 14, her diarrhea increased. Her temperature shot back up. She became unresponsive, and she remained that way until she died.

Felicia introduced our hospital to Ebola.

Every shift, we would have to pull nurses away from their assignments and leave an area of the hospital short-staffed. One case of Ebola had strained our staff. I could not imagine what it would be like if we experienced an outbreak.

Our nurses who cared for Felicia were courageous and compassionate. They were the first to treat an Ebola patient at ELWA Hospital, and they took great care of Felicia.

They also encouraged their colleagues to sign up for shifts in the unit. The work had not been as bad as they expected. Their chief complaint was that it was hot inside the suits, with no air conditioning in a high-humidity environment. But other than that, treating an Ebola patient was a job that they had discovered they could do.

We had one nurse who experienced a problem with her asthma being exacerbated by the masks we had to wear. But all the rest who worked in the unit volunteered to do so again.

Everyone in the country was scared of this Ebola thing. But the nurses who went into the unit to care for Felicia realized that more than dealing with a disease, we were dealing with a person who needed compassion.

A PERFECT STORM

The fight against Ebola felt like a race in which the starter forgot to say "On your mark" and "Get set" and skipped directly to "Go!"

In late March, Doctors Without Borders had launched an emergency response due to the Ebola cases that had popped up in Guinea, which borders Liberia to the north. Doctors Without Borders, which is better known internationally by its French acronym of MSF (*Médecins Sans Frontières*), was created by French doctors in 1971 as a humanitarian organization to provide emergency medical aid around the world. MSF is normally the first organization on the ground to identify and respond to outbreaks such as the Ebola epidemic in Guinea.

MSF had been successful in containing previous Ebola occurrences. There had been fewer than twenty Ebola episodes since the virus was identified in 1976 in two simultaneous events—one in Sudan and another in Zaire (now the Democratic Republic of Congo), in a village near the Ebola River. MSF's quick responses had prevented these prior outbursts from becoming widespread. The most deaths from an Ebola outbreak had been 280 in Zaire in 1976.

This time, however, MSF recognized the perfect storm gathering for a potential catastrophe with this reappearance of Ebola, which had begun in a very mobile society within a tri-border region where the virus had not previously appeared. Thus, the people in that area were not on the lookout for it. Guinea, Sierra Leone, and Liberia also were three of the poorest countries in the world, and general distrust of government caused the people to argue that Ebola was not a real virus, that it didn't actually exist.

For all those reasons, MSF knew it would be extremely difficult to bring a West African outbreak under control.

I had been working at ELWA Hospital on the south side of Monrovia for only eight months when we admitted Felicia. SIM ran the Eternal Love Winning Africa (ELWA) mission in Liberia, where it had maintained a presence since it started Radio ELWA in 1952. SIM had also opened a hospital in 1965 on its 130-acre compound that became known collectively as ELWA, or E-L-W-A. Monrovians consider ELWA like a section or neighborhood of the city.

Amber and I had signed up for a two-year term at ELWA through World Medical Mission, the medical arm of Samaritan's Purse, which offers terms in mission hospitals to young doctors like me who want to pursue medical mission work on a lifelong basis. Samaritan's Purse, named for the good Samaritan in Luke 10 who rescued a dying man that others had walked past and ignored, was created in 1970 to offer care to the poor and suffering in crisis areas around the world.

Samaritan's Purse and SIM had been working side by side in various efforts to assist the people of Liberia in their recovery from two civil wars in the previous twenty-five years.

Liberia (meaning "liberty") began as an American settlement in the 1820s by the American Colonization Society. Free blacks and, later, rescued slaves from illegal trade ships came to the west coast of Africa. In 1847 they signed a declaration of independence and founded the Republic of Liberia, modeling their constitution after that of the United States. American settlers, of course, were not the first people to live there, so immediate tension and distrust grew between the settlers and the local tribal groups.

Perhaps it was due to this tension that, over one hundred years later in 1980, an indigenous leader, Samuel Doe, rose to power through a coup and the slaughtering of the president and his cabinet. Through fraudulent elections, Doe named himself president and began a bloody and racially charged rule. In 1989, a rebel leader, Charles Taylor, overthrew Doe's government and Liberia's civil war ensued. More than two hundred thousand Liberian lives were lost in the war, and a million more were displaced as refugees.

Finally, in 2003, largely through the courage and determination of Liberia's women and mothers, Charles Taylor was forced to resign and a peace accord was signed. Taylor was later indicted for crimes against humanity. The United Nations Mission in Liberia (UNMIL) came to monitor the peace accord. Then in 2005, Africa's first female president was elected, President Ellen Johnson Sirleaf, or "Ma Ellen" as she is called by her people.

The needs of the Liberians were many and great, and we were there not to be Westerners swooping in to do things our way or to make them like us, but to partner with the Liberians as they helped themselves. Our hospital's medical director, Dr. Brown, is Liberian and a very influential medical voice in his country. We also worked with a team of general practitioners and nurses from Liberia.

Dr. Debbie, a general surgeon from Oregon, had moved to Liberia a year earlier and headed up ELWA Hospital's Ebola response. She sent the medical staff an e-mail on March 22 informing us of a news report that up to fifty-nine people in Guinea had died from the rare and deadly Ebola Virus Disease. The article also reported that Ebola might have spread to Sierra Leone, Liberia's neighbor to the northwest.

"I thought that you all would be interested in this," she wrote. "It is a bit close for comfort. We all need to be alert to the possibility of seeing something here."

Two days later, we held our first doctors' meeting about Ebola to discuss how we would combat the disease if it made it into our country and city.

I knew about Ebola from my medical education when we studied rare, exotic viruses like Ebola, Lassa fever, and Hantavirus. I knew it was a really bad, viral, hemorrhagic fever with no cure, no vaccine, and an astoundingly high death rate.

In 2013, during my residency training, I had spent three weeks in Uganda at Mulago Hospital. They had treated a patient with Ebola the month before our arrival, and there had been other cases in Uganda. Signs around the hospital kept patients and medical personnel on alert for symptoms of the disease: "Do you have a fever?" "Are you bleeding?" "Do you have Ebola?" That level of public awareness had helped minimize the outbreak in East Africa.

But when we moved to Liberia in October 2013, there had been no documented cases—ever—of Ebola in West Africa. Ebola was not on my radar; I did not expect to see it there.

We might be overreacting a bit because Guinea is a long way from here, I thought when our discussion began. It was 282 miles from Monrovia to the city of Foya near the Guinea border. After just a few minutes of Dr. Debbie and Dr. John Fankhauser describing the situation, though, I changed my mind and agreed that we needed to take immediate action. We absolutely had to prepare for the worst.

We brainstormed where we could create a safe space to isolate a patient. That place wound up being our chapel, a small, freestanding building in the courtyard of the horseshoe-shaped hospital. Our staff devotionals were held each morning in the chapel, along with afternoon discipleship classes for hospital employees.

Dr. Brown and Dr. Fankhauser received pushback on their decision to isolate Ebola patients in the chapel. Some were upset the chapel would be used for such a dirty job and that we would be bringing death into a sacred place.

Jerry and John explained the move by asking, historically, in times of war, where had people gone for refuge? They went to churches, Jerry and John said, and what better place could we offer than a chapel to bring sick patients who were in search of life?

Work began immediately to convert the chapel into an isolation unit, which we called the Case Management Center, with five beds and a small area for storage.

The doctors' meeting regarding the Ebola threat took place on the twenty-fourth of March, a Monday. I had recently been named physician liaison for the HIV treatment program and spent three days that week in meetings at the National AIDS Control Program for staff in all of Liberia's HIV clinics. Ebola was on my mind so often during those meetings that I downloaded the Twitter app on my phone and created an account so I could follow Ebola updates from the World Health Organization (WHO), the Centers for Disease Control and Prevention (CDC), and UNMIL.

At ELWA we began implementing strict universal precautions regarding contact with potential Ebola patients based on a 1998 WHO booklet titled "Infection Control for Viral Haemorrhagic Fevers in the African Health Care Setting" that we found online.

The best science we knew at the time said Ebola was transmitted through body fluids, such as sweat, blood, vomit, and diarrhea. As far as viruses were concerned, Ebola did not spread easily. It required direct exposure to mucous membrane (eyes, nose, mouth) or broken skin (a cut or even a small scratch or scrape).

By comparison, Ebola was not spread through coughing, as with measles or influenza. When we cough, our breath contains tiny particles that can travel across a room on air currents. Ebola was transmitted only via droplets, which by definition are larger particles. Because of the weight of droplets, gravity prevents them from becoming airborne.

Ebola may not be easily transmissible, but its greatest threat comes in needing only a small amount of virus to cause infection. The medical term *viral load* refers to the number of copies of a virus in a milliliter of bodily fluid. Ebola has one of the highest viral loads among viruses. With HIV, for example, 100,000 copies per milliliter is a high viral load. In an Ebola patient near death, the number of copies of the virus in one milliliter can reach into the billions. Additionally, it takes a relatively small number of Ebola viral particles to cause infection. I have heard estimates of 10 to 1,000. When you consider that a dying patient can have upwards of a billion particles in one milliliter of bodily fluid, it is easy to understand the danger inherent with Ebola.

To use a military analogy, most viruses would be like a nation with a poorly trained force that needs to deploy its entire army into enemy territory to complete a mission. Ebola, though, would be like a terrorist cell that only needs two or three terrorists to infiltrate to inflict deadly damage.

Health-care workers are disproportionately affected by the virus for a couple of reasons.

First, they provide care to very sick infected patients. Ebola is not easily transmitted in the early stages of the illness. But as the patients become sicker, their viral load increases.

A good example of that is the case of Thomas Eric Duncan, the Liberian who in September 2014 became the first person to be diagnosed with Ebola in the United States. He was with his family in the first days of his illness, but none of them contracted Ebola. The two people who became infected through contact with him were nurses who cared for him as his sickness worsened.

Second, health-care workers encounter patients before they are known to have Ebola. Especially early in the West Africa outbreak, patients would come into an emergency room or a clinic with symptoms commonly ascribed to malaria. The medical personnel first seeing those patients often did not have all the proper personal protective equipment and were not able to follow certain procedures to prevent Ebola's spread.

Therefore, one of the keys to preventing an epidemic is to first ensure the safety and preparedness of medical workers.

On High Alert

Kent

Ebola had never before struck a highly populated area. That changed when Ebola came to Guinea.

In addition to bordering Liberia to the north, Guinea wraps north and west around Sierra Leone, like an umbrella. Ebola cases had first appeared in southeast Guinea. Then we received word of confirmed cases in the capital city of Conakry on the country's western coast, as well as suspected cases to the north. In a short time the virus had made a huge geographical leap from the southeast part of Guinea to its west coast and possibly to its north.

Until then every Ebola outbreak had occurred in a rural village. In Conakry, with more than 1.6 million people, the virus had emerged for the first time in a densely populated city.

During that time, the virus also made its first appearance in Liberia, in the northern town of Foya, which sits across the borders from both Guinea and Sierra Leone.

One female patient with the virus left Foya and came down to Monrovia via taxi. That woman's sister had contracted the disease in Guinea, and she had brought her sister into Liberia for medical care. Her sister died at the border, but the woman traveled on to Monrovia via taxi with four other passengers. Her husband lived at Firestone, a district near Roberts International Airport, which is a forty-minute drive southeast of ELWA. When the woman started feeling ill, she caught a ride on a motorcycle taxi to the hospital in Firestone.

The woman wound up being isolated and later died, along with her young child and, I believe, her husband. When we were told in a meeting that she had Ebola and that there were potentially eighty contacts, I knew the disease was about to erupt.

We determined that if the situation began to deteriorate, we would evacuate the medical missionaries' spouses and children because of their close contact.

I left the meeting thinking of Marion, our housekeeper. She came and went every day from our house, and I kept thinking about those eighty contacts around Monrovia who had been exposed. *Where in the community had Marion been? With whom had she had contact in the community? Was she in danger of becoming infected? Had she already been infected with the virus?*

On March 31, we provided a Samaritan's Purse representative with our families' names, dates of birth, passport numbers, and evacuation destinations, just in case they needed to be hurried out of the country.

That same day, the last patient I saw in the clinic reported having suffered for a couple of days from fever, a headache, body aches, and chills—classic symptoms of malaria. I sent him to the lab for a malaria test and told him I would take his chart to the emergency room, and that he should go there from the lab because the clinic would be closing soon. At the ER, they would review his lab results and give him the prescription he needed. I then went to a 6 p.m. meeting about Ebola.

During the meeting, as we received the latest updates, my thoughts kept going back to my last patient. *I didn't ask what he does for a living,* I realized. *What if he was the motorcycle taxi driver?*

I left the meeting and walked to the ER. I asked the doctor on duty, "Did you see this guy from the clinic whom I sent over to the lab?"

"No," he answered. "We haven't seen him."

There was a stack of charts on the desk, and I flipped through them until I found my patient's. There were no lab results and no notes from the ER doctor. I asked again if the man had been there.

"No. You brought the chart over here, but we never saw him."

I went to the lab and asked who had performed the blood draw on the patient. No one seemed to know. We began looking through two boxes filled with little squares of paper with every lab result from the day. None bore the man's name.

I went back to the chart, then called the phone number that the man had given us. The call did not go through, as if the number was disconnected.

What if I just missed the first case of Ebola at ELWA? I just examined him. I didn't wear gloves, and he was all sweaty.

I am not the type to get paranoid, but in that moment I was. I called John Fankhauser and detailed the situation. We thought through every good and bad scenario we could. Most likely, the man had malaria. But we could not know that for sure. Who was that man? Could he have been one of those eighty contacts?

I considered not going home that night in case I had been exposed to the virus. John reassured me that it would be okay to be around my family, because the incubation period for Ebola is two to twenty-one days. I would not get sick the same day, and if I had no symptoms, I would not be contagious.

Amber

That evening Kent explained what had happened at the hospital, and we had a serious discussion about the rapidly changing situation in Monrovia. I could see that Ebola was coming to where we lived, and specifically to where Kent worked. He described all the protocols in place at the hospital and his confidence in them. We both grasped the serious nature of what we sensed was beginning.

We didn't believe that because we were there as medical missionaries we would automatically be divinely protected from getting Ebola. The Bible says, "For God has not given us a spirit of fear and timidity, but of power, love, and self-discipline."[1] Although Ebola is a scary disease, we were not scared. We were not afraid of dying. Missionaries have died on their chosen fields for centuries, and before going into Liberia we had prepared our wills. We also had placed a letter on file with Samaritan's Purse to be given to our parents in the case of our deaths, reassuring them of our confidence in the work we had gone there to do.

The circumstances in Liberia had changed since we had arrived, but this was still exactly what we had signed up for. We talked that night about why we were there in the first place, and we went to bed unsure of what would happen in the coming days, weeks, or months, yet also with complete peace.

Kent

The next morning as I made my walk to work, I again dialed the cell phone number from my patient's chart. This time the phone rang and he answered.

"How are you doing?" I asked.

"Oh, I am trying. I am trying." In Liberia that is like saying "I am okay."

He told me that he had not gone to the lab because he did not have the money with him to pay, so he went home to get it and would be coming back to the lab that day to be tested.

"Please do, please do," I begged him.

"I am not worse," he said. "I am about the same."

He came into the lab that morning and tested positive for malaria.

Malaria is no fun, but at least it is treatable. I was relieved to learn his diagnosis, that I had not missed our first Ebola case after all. I had not been exposed through my ungloved hands.

That was our hospital's baptism—we realized how quickly Ebola could pop up, and we knew the safety precautions we needed to take.

On April 1, because of the imminent threat of Ebola in Monrovia, Samaritan's Purse made the decision to begin evacuating families. We purchased plane tickets for Amber and our two kids, Ruby, age five, and Stephen, age three. A day later, they flew out of Liberia.

Amber

The return flight on our tickets was in three weeks, but that was a changeable date. We did not know when we would be going back to Liberia other than that it would be after the country had been Ebola free for a full incubation period of twenty-one days.

The kids and I went to stay with my parents in Abilene, Texas, where I was able to visit with all six of my siblings. We also attended a family reunion in Alabama on Kent's side of the family. While we were there, we were able to see Kent's cousin, Stephen, and his wife, Amy, and their new baby. Since they also were missionaries (to Zambia), it was a special treat to see them.

But I really wanted to be back in Liberia. Although we hadn't been there six months yet, Liberia had become our home. Our work was there. Our people were there.

Stephen and Ruby missed their dad a lot too. We were able to FaceTime with Kent almost every day, which helped, but it wasn't the same as being there with him.

There were no new cases of Ebola in Monrovia, so I wasn't concerned about Kent in that regard. But I did not like him being alone. He was working long hours to begin with, and the speed with which Ebola had become a threat to Monrovia created tension and anxiety in the hospital that were difficult for him to work under.

So while I enjoyed being with my family in the States, my desire was for the kids and me to return as soon as possible to Kent in Liberia.

OUTBREAK AVERTED

Kent

Through April and into May, I think everyone at the hospital was running on adrenaline. Everything seemed to be happening all at once.

Over a two-week period, we put our entire staff through training on how to deal with Ebola. We covered every topic from "What is Ebola?" to "How to manage a dead body." We mixed bleach solution every day for use around the hospital. With the nature of the virus, there was no margin for error. One small mistake—just a piece of skin exposed—could prove deadly.

Converting the chapel into the isolation unit was a total team effort. The teenage children of missionaries worked with SIM's service workers to build fences, dig latrines, and bring running water into the future unit.

Samaritan's Purse provided equipment and supplies to stock the unit. Dr. Debbie dug through supplies in the pharmacy storehouse that had not yet been processed and found several boxes of scrubs. Those were hauled to the chapel porch, and when we had time, we sorted the scrubs by sizes and got them washed and folded.

Ed Carns, a physician in his seventies from Oklahoma, arrived in late April to be an extra pair of hands in the hospital. With Amber and the kids gone, Ed stayed with me for a week.

Ed is a happy guy who just has a natural ability—a gift, actually—to encourage people. He laughs a lot, and although we were not spending many hours at home during that stretch, we enjoyed our time together. Ed brought fresh cheer into a stressful situation, and we bonded during our time together.

We had that one case of the woman with Ebola who had traveled from Foya through Monrovia to Firestone, but none of the hospitals in the city had received an Ebola patient. Up in Foya, there turned out to be only a handful of cases, and they all were residents of Guinea who had crossed the border seeking medical care. MSF had set up an isolation unit in Foya and successfully isolated the patients.

The last new case reported in Foya came in mid-April. When the twenty-one-day incubation period ended in May, those of us at ELWA breathed a collective sigh of relief. A widespread outbreak in the country had been averted.

Before the arrival of Ebola, our family had planned to go to Greece in late April for the Christian Medical and Dental Associations' annual Continuing Medical and Dental Education Conference, always an important event for medical missionaries. I was scheduled to assist there in teaching an emergency obstetrics course, and Dr. Debbie also had planned to attend.

Before leaving for the conference, we had to check with MSF officials to determine whether we could travel to the conference because of the small Ebola outbreak. Their guidelines called for workers who have had contact with Ebola patients to stay within four hours of a hospital with isolation capabilities, to monitor their temperatures daily, and to follow a detailed protocol if they began feeling poorly or developed a fever. Since we had not cared for any patients with Ebola, we were in the clear.

I met Amber, Ruby, and Stephen in London, and we flew to Greece together. It was good to see them, but it remained a stressful time. Living in a hotel for a week and a half presents its own challenges, and it was still uncertain whether Amber and the kids would be able to return to Liberia. While we were in Greece, SP Liberia gave the all clear for Amber and the kids to return, and so we did—eagerly anticipating a return to life as normal.

THE ANGRY MOB

Near the end of May, our facility was awaiting direction from Liberia's Ministry of Health concerning our request to take down the temporary isolation unit we had set up in our hospital. We had passed forty-two days since the last new case of Ebola had been reported in the country, which is two complete incubation periods.

We had planned for our isolation unit to serve only as a holding area, not a treatment center. If a patient tested positive, we would transfer him for treatment at John F. Kennedy Medical Center (JFK), the large government-run hospital in Monrovia.

But when Dr. Brown asked the Ministry of Health about taking down our unit, we did not know that JFK's isolation unit had already been disassembled and all the equipment moved into storage. Jerry was told that the person responsible for making the decision regarding our unit was out of the country and that we should keep ours in place in the interim.

Late on the evening of Saturday, May 31, a very sick patient came into our ER, and I diagnosed him with acute pyelonephritis with sepsis, a bad kidney infection with pus in the kidney. We began treatment with lots of fluid and IV antibiotics. As we gave the patient more fluid, he failed to produce any urine, causing me to believe he also had acute renal failure. That was difficult to treat, because we still had to give him fluid due to his being septic and having slightly low blood pressure.

Sometimes when taking a weekend call shift from Saturday to Monday, I would go home at night to get a couple hours of sleep. But with this critically ill patient in the ER and other patients on the ward to tend to, I stayed at the hospital all night, checking on them frequently.

During the night the man developed a facial twitch. I checked his potassium level, which I found was dangerously high. We began treating him with glucose and insulin, because that was the only means we had to lower his potassium levels quickly. His twitching continued and turned into jerking. I ordered the nurse to give him diazepam (Valium) to sedate him and make him more comfortable. Later on I noticed bleeding from his diazepam injection sites. When his twitching and jerking resumed, he also began bleeding from his mouth, tongue, and gums. It was obvious that something was out of the ordinary, and it appeared that he might be nearing the end of his life. There was nothing more we could do—no cardiac monitoring, no dialysis, no vasopressors, no ventilator available.

Sunday morning, another patient came in with what I determined to be eclampsia with a breech baby and a bleeding placenta previa—three diagnoses that each would have been challenging on its own. I called Dr. Debbie, our general surgeon, and asked her to back me up on a C-section in case we needed to perform a cesarean hysterectomy. Dr. Debbie and I were sitting in the operating room while the patient was being prepped, and I told her about the difficult case in the ER and the possibility that he could have something different, and that I was beginning to feel paranoid that he could have Ebola.

"Then let's take action," she said.

We went to the ER and it was obvious that the man was dying, and there were no interventions we could perform to save his life. He was in a corner bed by the back door, and we instructed the nurses to put curtains around him and not to touch him, not to let anyone near him, and not to let anyone use the back door.

During the surgery on the pregnant woman—which turned out to be a completely uneventful procedure with both the mother and the baby coming out fine—the man in the ER died.

Wearing full PPE, we wheeled the deceased in his bed out the back door of the ER and through the grass to a tent we had established as a place to triage patients suspicious for Ebola.

We ordered the ER decontaminated with the bleach-water mixture, while we wrapped his body in several plastic sheets, spraying each layer of sheets and his bed with the mixture. We alerted the Ministry of Health that we had a suspicious death, possibly from Ebola, so that they could draw a postmortem blood sample.

It took the Ministry of Health more than twenty-four hours to come take that sample, then it would be another day before the results came back.

The man's family was cooperative, but Tuesday afternoon—as word spread that the body was still at the hospital—a large crowd gathered outside the compound wall. The crowd grew more restless and angry, demanding that the man's body be released to be prepared properly and buried in a timely fashion, according to their custom. Dr. John Fankhauser called me at home to tell me that he was going to release the body to the family.

John and I are close friends with a great working relationship. As is typical with doctors, we do not always agree with each other's opinions, and when we do disagree, we let each other know about it and professionally discuss our differences. Ultimately, when it comes to decision time, we respect and abide by whoever's decision it is to make. Whether we agree or not, it becomes *our* decision.

I disagreed with John's wanting to release the body without the results of the Ebola test, so I headed toward the hospital.

When I saw the angry crowd, I went around through a back entrance to where John was suited up in PPE and preparing the body for the family. He had told them that if they would bring a coffin, he would have the body put into the coffin and given to them.

"I'm not comfortable with this decision," I told John. "Why are we doing this?"

"Because they're threatening to kill us," he said. "They're threatening to burn down the hospital and kill all of us, and it's not worth it."

Four or five of us suited up in PPE to help John place the body in the coffin, and a Ministry of Health official showed up and said he wanted to meet with the family. The patient had tested positive for Lassa fever, which is endemic in West

Africa and typically spread through rat droppings and rat urine. There are between 300,000 and 500,000 cases per year. Most Lassa fever patients have either no symptoms or mild ones and recover on their own. But 10 to 20 percent of cases require hospitalization, and among those the mortality rate is 50 percent.

After the family had met with the Ministry of Health, we pulled back the plastic sheets enough so that two family members could see their loved one's face to identify the body. We placed the body in the coffin, sprayed everything with bleach, and closed the coffin. Even though the patient did not have Ebola, it was necessary to practice such caution, because in severe cases of Lassa fever, there can be human-to-human transmission.

The family members went back outside the hospital wall to the crowd, and when they appeared without the body, the crowd went crazy. I heard the *bang* of something hitting the big metal gate. Then rocks started flying over the wall. The crowd was throwing gravel and rocks at the hospital! We were standing twenty to thirty yards from the gate, so we were not in any kind of danger, but rocks splashed in puddles in front of us before we backed farther out of range.

A hospital janitor, also in PPE, was standing with us. "Prince," I asked him, "have you seen anything like this before?"

"No, I haven't," Prince said as he looked down at his suit. "I had never heard of PPE before we took Dr. Debbie's class."

"No," I told him, "I'm talking about an angry mob throwing rocks at a hospital."

"Oh yeah," Prince replied with a chuckle. "I see that all the time."

The police were called and the crowd quickly dispersed. Then the Ministry of Health brought in a truck, loaded the coffin, and took it for burial where the family wanted.

Even though that patient did not have Ebola, that case put us on high alert . . . and turned out to be the beginning of our Ebola scare.

One week later, Felicia and her uncle came to our hospital.

PART 2

CALLED TO SERVE

3

She Said "Yes"

Kent

W hen the going gets tough, the tough go back to their calling." I knew I had to write those words into my journal as soon as I heard them, because they came from Ken Lloyd, a man who had spent almost fifty years in cross-cultural mission work.

Amber and I had started our mission commitment five months earlier in Monrovia. It was mid-March 2014, and we were at a conference for Liberian missionaries associated with SIM. The three-day retreat, on the West African coast at Libassa, offered a time of team building, renewal, and encouragement for the missionary families.

The resort at Libassa was nestled into a palm forest, positioned perfectly between the Atlantic Ocean and a freshwater lagoon. The scenery was some of God's most beautiful creative work, found right in the middle of a war-scarred, majority-world country. And it was to Liberia that Amber and I had been called, to serve some of God's most beautiful people suffering in a nation with wounds still obvious from not one but two civil wars within the last generation.

The theme of the main session centered on our callings as missionaries, and when the speaker said, "When the going gets tough, the tough go back to their calling," I wrote that down verbatim, because I expected tough times would someday come our way.

I did not know how soon they would come.

Or how tough the going would get.

Not that the threat of Ebola, or any other unforeseen circumstances, would have changed anything. Amber and I were not in Liberia because we had arbitrarily chosen to move there. There was a calling on our lives to go to Liberia, and we were there because we had determined to be obedient to God's invitation.

No matter how tough it got.

PILOT, ASTRONAUT, COWBOY . . . MISSIONARY

I began to sense the prompting of God into foreign service while attending Abilene Christian University (ACU) in Texas. I started out as an undecided major, and I was about as undecided about my future as a college freshman can be. I had grown up with lots of interests and liked a variety of subjects in school. Along the way, I wanted to become a pilot, an astronaut, and then a cowboy. My dad was a doctor, and I respected his profession. But deep in my heart, the way I wanted to be like my dad was as a good husband, father, and church leader—not a physician.

During my first year at ACU in 1999, I felt pressure to choose a major and took part in career counseling to help determine what I wanted to be when I grew up. I chose to be a high-school math teacher and coach, largely because my high-school math teacher was also my soccer coach, and he had led groups on summer mission trips. I thought that sounded like a life I would enjoy.

My first semester as a sophomore, I took math and education classes. Calculus and the education courses had me rethinking my newly declared major. The next semester, I took part in ACU's Study Abroad Program in Oxford, England. Dr. Paul Morris, a physics and philosophy professor, accompanied us for the semester, and I signed up for his Introduction to Philosophy and his History and Philosophy of Science courses.

My favorite class in England was Christian Worship, in which we studied the history of worship in various Christian traditions. For that class we were required to visit seven types of Christian churches and interview someone at each church about their worship service and their traditions and liturgy. Observing the different manners of worship and interviewing people about their expressions of faith fascinated me.

At the end of the semester in Oxford, I still did not know what career I wanted to pursue, but I did possess a deepening desire to learn from the great biblical scholars and theologians at ACU, as well as to study the Bible more on my own. I switched my major to Biblical Text, which offered studies on the Bible's language, message, and historical context. It was a common major for students who planned to become preachers. I wasn't necessarily preparing to become a preacher or Bible teacher, although those were options, but I figured that at some point over the next couple of years, I would discover what I was meant to do in life.

The degree plan called for an internship in Christian service between my junior and senior years. I had the choice to work with young people in Atlanta, Georgia, or go to East Africa with a friend to help with his internship. For some reason, serving people in East Africa sounded more up my alley than youth work in the United States.

While in East Africa, I began to sense my life calling. It wasn't for the type of mission work I was most familiar with, though, because growing up in church and hearing missionaries speak, what I'd heard them say most concerned preaching, teaching, and planting churches in foreign countries. I did not consider myself skilled as a preacher or a teacher—getting up to speak in front of people was not in my comfort zone. But I did know that I could show compassion to people in need.

My favorite Bible quote is found in the book of Mark. It is part of the story of Jesus taking five loaves of bread and two fish and miraculously feeding five thousand people. The context is that the twelve apostles had just returned to Jesus after he had sent them out in pairs to physically heal people, as well as explain to them the meaning of the kingdom of God. Then Jesus learned that King Herod had ordered the beheading of John the Baptist, the prophet and cousin of Jesus who had baptized him at the beginning of Jesus's ministry.

I try to imagine the emotional weight of that moment on Jesus, with this great tragedy saddled right up next to the excitement and joy of the returning apostles sharing stories of their magnificent accomplishments on Jesus's behalf.

Jesus had to be exhausted as a large crowd of people began to gather, and he told the apostles to go away with him to a quiet place where they could rest. Jesus and the disciples got into a boat and crossed the lake, but as Mark's account explains, the people ran ahead around the lake shore and were waiting for Jesus on the other side when his boat landed. That leads to my favorite Bible verse, Mark 6:34: "When Jesus landed and saw a large crowd, *he had compassion on them,* because they were like sheep without a shepherd. So he began teaching them many things."

When I am emotionally exhausted, I become irritable, short-tempered, and snappy. My natural tendency, if I had been in Jesus's boat with him, would have been to greet the people with, "Are you kidding me? We are trying to get away from you people! Give us a break!"

But not Jesus. His response, in that moment with all the weight on him and the exhaustion he was experiencing, was to feel compassion for the people and to teach them. Why? Because he saw that the people needed help; in his time and place they were sheep in need of a shepherd.

Jesus put aside his own feelings and saw their needs. He taught them, then he fed them. He took care of both their spiritual need and their physical need. The two always went hand in hand with Jesus.

I wanted to feel that kind of compassion for others. I wanted to see and meet others' spiritual and physical needs.

∞

While on that internship in East Africa, I thought about my abilities, interests, and experiences. In the end, I decided I wanted to go to medical school so I could become a doctor and use those skills to serve people on the mission field. Having grown up in a doctor's home, becoming a physician did not seem an unreachable goal to me.

Initially, I thought that on my vacations from my medical practice in America, I would visit friends who were missionaries in foreign countries and offer medical care to them and their families, because that was a need I knew missionaries had. But as God's calling for me began to take root, it matured into something bigger. I began to realize that I needed to use my life—not just my vacation time—in this kind of service.

My career choice was never about the pursuit of becoming a doctor. My goal was to find a way to serve people, and medicine was a career through which I could live a life of service.

TASTE OF MISSIONS

Amber

I wanted to be a nurse as far back as I can remember. I didn't have any nurses or doctors in my family, and I didn't know what nurses did, other than give shots. But I had watched the movie *Florence Nightingale,* starring Jaclyn Smith, as a young girl, and that movie inspired me to want to be a nurse so I could help other people just like Florence Nightingale did.

I broke my arm when I was eight years old, and as I was being tended to by nurses following surgery, my dad tried to encourage me, saying, "Someday when you are a nurse, Amber Joy, you may take care of a little girl with a broken arm. And you will better be able to take care of her, because you will know what it feels like to have a broken arm."

My parents laid a foundation of faith and caring for other people early in my life. My dad was a preacher, and for five years we lived in a poor town in Colorado. We weren't missionaries, but I think my parents viewed what they did there as mission work.

We lived in Oklahoma, Colorado, and central Texas when I was growing up, and most of those years, we would make a couple of trips per year to the Texas-Mexico border to visit a missionary family our church supported. I loved the family, I loved visiting them, I loved going into Mexico with them, and I loved the Spanish language. Based on our visits, I thought all missionaries preached, did school programs to teach the Bible to children, dug latrines, and occasionally constructed new church buildings. It was a narrow view of what missions truly is, but I still thought it was cool.

The summer after my high-school graduation, our family made another trip to visit our missionary friends, and when it was time to return home, I wanted to stay. I begged my dad to let me remain there for two more weeks before starting college at Abilene Christian, but he talked me into going back home with our family. I reluctantly obeyed.

During my first semester at ACU in 2002, I signed up for the first trip available for mission service in another country. It was supposed to be a two-week, summertime trip to Honduras with other nursing and pre-med students, but I raised enough funds to commit to a two-month internship. By the time of our trip, I had become a certified nursing assistant, which required learning common medical terms and how to assist a nurse.

On that trip, I observed for the first time how a nurse could be a missionary and—I was *so* naive!—noted that because there already were nurses doing such work, I wouldn't have to be the pioneer nursing missionary and figure out how to make it work.

Two significant experiences occurred during that trip.

First, earlier in the summer, I had taught at a children's Bible school in Limón. Kids from several neighboring towns and villages came by bus with their parents to participate in a big gathering of regional churches. I helped the kids learn a song in Spanish that included the words "Jesus is my friend."

Five weeks later, the medical team and I went out to a village a good bus ride from where I had worked at the Bible school. When I got out of the truck, a group of kids recognized me and came running, singing, *"Mi amigo, Jesús es mi amigo."* It moved me to realize that a song I had taught those kids had stuck with them. Even if it turned out that was the only thing they recalled from the Bible school, what a great thing to remember: "Jesus is my friend"!

That was an affirming moment for me in feeling my own life call to long-term medical missions.

The other significant experience that summer was meeting a tall, slender, good-looking young man who had come to Honduras on a mission trip with his church.

Kent Brantly had just completed his bachelor's degree and was trying to determine whether he should attempt to get into medical school. He spent a few days with us working at the medical clinic, and I taught him how to measure blood pressure. I let him put the cuff on me so many times that my arms were turning purple and I thought they might fall off. But I was willing to risk that to spend time with Kent.

The day we met, we ate fried fish and rice with tongue depressors because we didn't have any spoons. We did not know it then, but that was exactly the kind of experience that a life in medical missions would offer.

Kent

On that trip to Honduras, I was sitting in a small church building with a nurse practitioner who was the medical missionary there. Among the patients was one elderly lady who didn't really have anything we could treat. All we gave her were vitamins and Tylenol, but she was so appreciative and thankful that we had cared for her. Something about that interaction moved me, and I thought, *This just feels right. I think I can do this.*

I returned to ACU for a fifth year to take all my science prerequisites needed to apply to medical school. I lived off campus that year, but Amber and I would see each other around the school.

LOVE IS PATIENT . . .

Amber

One day Kent invited me to come watch his niece's Under 11 soccer team that he coached, and when I showed up there I found that Kent had also invited another female friend. I obviously had read more into the invitation than Kent intended.

Kent's sister Carole also attended the game, and she couldn't believe that he had invited both me and the other girl. Kent likes being around people, and he was just being a nice guy inviting friends to come watch, not realizing that just about every girl at ACU would have gone to watch an Under 11 soccer game if it meant getting to spend part of a Saturday with him.

Not long after that day, he started dating the other girl he had invited. I had thought it would have been a nice story someday after we were married to tell how we had met in Honduras. My hopes for that were dashed.

We became better friends over my sophomore year, but not as good of friends as I had hoped. I worked at the campus store, and Kent would come in between classes to buy a pencil or Scantron card or something else he needed, and when he walked out, I would catch myself watching him leave. My co-workers knew how crazy I was about Kent, but he had no idea.

After Kent's fifth year at ACU, he returned to his hometown of Indianapolis to enter the Indiana University School of Medicine, and I continued my studies at ACU. We e-mailed each other occasionally just to stay in touch. I really loved Kent, and I would reach points where I would tell myself, *This has got to stop. I've got to move on.* But then he would send me an e-mail, sounding all chummy, and that would give me renewed hope until the next time I felt like I needed to give up on him.

Kent

In February 2007, during my second year of med school, Amber Joy—I like to call her that because her middle name describes her personality—sent me a birthday CD mix that she had put together from various songs she liked. Amber isn't a big lyrics person. She will like songs but not spend much time really listening to the words of the songs. I am the opposite; I pay attention to every word in a song.

I would listen to that CD in my car driving to and from school, as well as through headphones in the library. So I am hearing these songs over and over and over, and I'm paying attention to the words and noticing that some of the lyrics were pretty forward about being in love, about always loving someone, and about needing a wife.

I was in class or studying fifteen to eighteen hours a day and had not dated anyone in more than a year. When I looked around my classes, all I saw was a bunch of doctors-to-be, and with plans to become a doctor myself, I had zero interest in marrying another busy doctor. And if I wasn't going to marry someone, what was the point in dating her?

I started taking a mental inventory of every girlfriend I'd had—not to say there were a whole bunch, but there were a few—and every close female friend I'd had, and I thought about why I would not, could not, or should not marry each one. I had good reasons for all of them. Then I came to Amber Joy's name, and I could not come up with one reason why I had not dated her.

She was a godly young woman. She wanted to serve in missions. She had an awesome family. Not to mention I had spent several months listening to this CD she gave me with the not-so-subtle messages "I love you," "I'll always love you," and "You need a wife."

One day Amber e-mailed me about football. She had been a Denver Broncos fan her whole life and had never been to a game. They were not playing in Texas that season, but they were coming to Indianapolis in late September to play the Colts, and she wanted to know if I knew of someone she and her dad could stay with if they came to the game.

I am a big Colts fan and told her that she could stay at my parents' home, and that I would love to go the game with her and her dad. As the date of the game neared, her dad had to back out because he couldn't leave the church he pastored that weekend, and Amber asked if it would be okay if she came alone.

Amber flew in on Friday and spent Saturday with my mom grocery shopping and helping fill the pantry at our church. She had met an uncle and aunt of mine in Honduras and had stayed in contact with them, so we ate a meal with them. That was my aunt Joan who, seemingly every time the subject of girls came up, would say, "You know, Kent, that Amber Joy, she is a special girl."

"I know, Aunt Joan," I'd respond. "I know she's special."

We also had a sushi dinner with two of my friends. It was almost like a double date, although none of us would dare admit it was a date.

Amber

My Broncos lost on Sunday, but I got over it pretty quickly because I was with Kent. Afterward, we went to dinner, then to Starbucks for coffee. There was tall, decorative grass in front of the Starbucks, and I picked a piece of grass and got a splinter in my finger. Kent dug the splinter out of my finger.

Then I spilled my entire peppermint hot chocolate all over the Starbucks floor. That was so embarrassing. I never was very good at dating, because I usually managed to mess up one thing almost every time. Technically we weren't on a date, but I made more than my one mistake anyway.

Kent was gracious to me the entire time, overlooking the catastrophic spill, opening doors for me, and being a true gentleman. I got the guts to ask if he had a girlfriend, and he said he didn't.

I had taken a long weekend off from work so I was able to attend classes with him on Monday. We were in a radiology class that Kent really liked, and the professor was putting pictures up on a screen and asking questions about them. Only once did Kent raise his hand to answer the professor's questions, but after every question he leaned toward me and whispered the correct answer. I was so impressed!

Kent drove me to the airport later that day, and when it was time to say goodbye, Kent told me, "It was a lot of fun. See you later."

No hug. No kiss on the cheek. No grabbing my hand for a moment. Nothing. I was crushed!

MR. AND MRS. BRANTLY!

Kent

After Amber's visit, I grew more and more interested in her. My parents took my sister Krista and me to Hawaii for a medical conference. After the trip, I was going back to Abilene in December to visit Carole, and I knew that I would see Amber while I was in Abilene. I mailed Amber two postcards from Hawaii and bought her a Beanie hula bear and a Hawaiian necklace made of shells.

I landed in Abilene bearing gifts for Amber. It was near her birthday, and I also gave her Handel's *Messiah* on CD. (No mention of falling in love forever or needing a husband on that CD.)

I barely saw my sister and her family on that trip, spending most of the four days with Amber. One night one of her guy friends came over and we played games. I noticed he was very friendly with her. They were nothing more than friends, but being a guy, observing their interactions heightened my sense of urgency.

On my last night in Abilene, I arranged to meet up with Amber after having dinner with friends. I called my brother Kerry, who is my unofficial advisor and confidant.

"Kerry, I don't know what to do. I think I want to marry this girl."

"Well," he said, "that seems pretty straightforward."

"But I'm not dating her. I can't just ask her to marry me when we're not even dating. We don't even live in the same state."

"It will be interesting to see what you do," my wise advisor replied.

When I was with Amber in her car, she told me that she would be moving to California on January 1 for a three-month, travel nursing job. Then she informed me that a friend had told her that she had dreamed that Amber would meet a man in California and move to Mexico or Central America and never come back to the United States.

"I hope you don't go to California and meet somebody," I told her.

"Why not?" she asked.

"Because I like you, and I don't want you to meet anybody else."

"Really? I like you too."

I reached over and held her hand.

"I like you," I said, "and when I think about the future, I like the idea of you being in my future. But that is all I want to say about that."

End of conversation. I abruptly shut down that discussion, afraid to take it any further.

I returned home to Indiana with the understanding that we were dating. We talked on the phone every day for the next five or six months. She extended her contract in California to five months instead of three, and her contract ended at the same time as my third year of med school. She was planning to move back to Texas—thankfully her friend's dream had not come true—and I made plans to fly out to visit her.

We decided to take a trip together, going camping in Yosemite National Park, driving up to Oregon to visit my college roommate, and then taking Amber's possessions back to Texas.

I had begun making secret plans to ensure that Amber would be a permanent part of my future by asking her dad's permission to marry her and purchasing a ring. Making good use of the Internet, I scouted potential proposal sites at Yosemite, then reserved a campsite for us.

I flew into California on Sunday, May 18, and we set out for Yosemite the next day. We talked during the drive about our future. Although I had not yet proposed, we were talking seriously about marriage. Amber said there was no reason for us not to get married, and that she did not want to have a long engagement. I countered with every reason I could think of for waiting to marry. We had been dating only five months. We had dated long distance. I was in medical school and spending practically all my time either in class or studying. I didn't give her any hint that her dad had already given us his blessing, or that a proposal was coming soon.

We arrived at Yosemite early that afternoon and set up a separate tent for each of us. Then we drove into the valley to scope out the sights and make our plans for the next three days. Driving down into the park, we encountered long lines of traffic because of road construction. As we crawled along, I looked for a scenic, romantic place we could come back to the next day so that I could pop the question.

Tired of the traffic, we pulled into the parking lot for Bridalveil Fall and walked the easy hike down the trail. When we reached the base of the waterfall, a family was leaving. Amber and I were totally alone on a bright, sunshiny day at the base of this beautiful, 620-foot waterfall. A small rainbow arched above us from the mist of the waterfall. I thought of the weather forecast that called for cold and rain the rest of our stay.

This is my chance. I might not be in this situation again.

I got down on one knee and said, "Amber Joy, I love you and I want to spend the rest of my life with you. Will you marry me?"

She looked at me as if she were thinking, *Are you serious?*

Responding to her stunned silence, I added, "I have talked to your dad. And I do have a ring, but it's in my backpack in my tent."

"Of course!" Amber exclaimed.

Suddenly, every reason I had given her to postpone our marriage seemed insignificant. We called our families to tell them we were engaged and that we did not want to wait six months to get married. But I had to start back to school in two weeks. So Amber's mom began planning a wedding without the bride-to-be there.

We completed the rest of our planned trip, then on May 29, 2008, in Abilene, only ten days after I proposed, we married in an outdoor ceremony complete with two violinists, a professional photographer, a nice wedding cake, and enough fajita meat for our seventy-five guests. Among the guests were two friends from Indianapolis who had come in a pickup truck and took Amber's belongings ahead of us to our new home.

We got married on Thursday, and Monday morning I started my fourth year of medical school.

Some of my classmates knew I had planned to propose during our break. "How did it go?" they asked.

"She said 'Yes,'" I said. Then as I flashed my hand with the wedding ring on it, I added, "And 'I do.'"

Amber

And now I get to tell people the story of how we met in the mountains of Honduras!

4

A Whole New World

Kent

Amber and I did not simply choose to go Liberia. Instead, we decided to answer God's call on our lives to become medical missionaries. The difference seems small, but it is rather significant.

It was not like God showed up one day and told us he wanted us to move to Africa. That was just the next step in a long progression of choices toward obedience. Much earlier, we faced decisions of a seemingly different nature, like choosing to live within our means.

When I had served my internship in East Africa in 2002, I had worked with three different missionary teams in Kenya and Tanzania. I had thought that perhaps God would call me to spend the rest of my life as a missionary in Mwanza, Tanzania. Honestly, that did not appeal much to me.

I learned there how much I treasured my own personal and physical comfort. Throughout my month in Tanzania, every piece of furniture I sat on was wood or wicker with only a foam cushion for padding. I missed sinking my toes into plush carpet, slumping into a cushy chair, reclining in an aptly named La-Z-Boy, or stretching out for a nap on a soft couch.

After that trip, I took note of just how much I enjoyed comfort. The lesson learned sank in and reverberated, and my ears became more attuned whenever I heard someone talking about being willing to give up comfort to serve God.

I realized comfort had become an idol to me and I needed to sacrifice it. That did not mean I would start choosing the most difficult way to do things so I would always be uncomfortable, but it did mean not making decisions for the purpose of being comfortable.

That carried over into our marriage, where Amber and I made some of our big life decisions by intentionally choosing the less comfortable of our options. One of those big decisions was where we would live during my residency training after I graduated from medical school in 2009.

We had a really comfortable option if we stayed in Indiana, close to family in a middle-class community of people whose company we enjoyed. I would have had a good income for that area, and we could have bought a house there. Instead, we chose to move to Fort Worth, Texas, where we knew almost no one and would be about a three-hour drive from Amber's parents.

That also was the less comfortable option from a medical standpoint. John Peter Smith Hospital (JPS) in downtown Fort Worth was large and publicly funded by the county. It was a big program with a lot of people working there from diverse backgrounds and differing worldviews. The patient population would be more indigent than my Indiana option.

David McRay, who would become my fellowship director at JPS and a mentor and friend, offered great wisdom: a county hospital would be a great training ground for working in the majority of the world because I would learn how to work in an under-resourced system where what I needed would not always be available.

"You'll have to learn how to navigate a complicated system to help your patients get what they need," he advised me, "and if you can't handle the frustrations of doing that in this country in a county health system, then you probably can't handle the frustrations in a developing country where there is even less to work with."

Looking back, moving to an unfamiliar city and working in a county hospital did stretch us professionally and personally.

Amber and I, along with our infant daughter, Ruby, were living in a comfortable home in Fort Worth. In my first year of residency, which was our second year of marriage, we reviewed our budget and began to look for ways that we could better live within our means. We expected to be going into missions, and that would mean raising money to work in a foreign country. We did not want to have any unnecessary debt: we felt that being good stewards meant minimizing the amount of money we would need to raise for paying off debt we had accumulated during my medical training.

We decreased our spending everywhere we could. We downsized our cell-phone plans, we stopped eating out at restaurants, and we ate all the beans and rice we could muster. But our savings still were not adding up like we thought they should. The only thing we had not done was move out of our home.

We went to our church's financial-assistance committee and informed the members that we did not need help paying bills and did not need any cash, but we asked if we could show them our budget and receive their input on how better to live within our means. The committee members looked over our budget and agreed that there was nothing more we could practically cut other than our rent expenses.

I met with our landlord and explained our situation. I was hoping he would offer to renegotiate our rent, but he didn't. Instead, he said he understood what I needed to do for my family and graciously offered to let us move out whenever we wanted, free of penalty. About ten days later, we moved out of our comfortable rental house and into the home of some friends from church for a month before going to Guatemala for a month-long rotation. When we returned to Fort Worth, we stayed with our friends long enough to find an apartment within our new budget. To live within our means, we moved into a nine-hundred-square foot unit in a complex where many of the residents were receiving government subsidies.

Even some of our closest friends asked why we would move out of a house with a big yard to an apartment in a lower-income neighborhood. The reason was simple: comfort was not the most important thing to us. We needed to be responsible with our finances and not accrue more debt. We lived in that apartment for the next three years, enjoyed our stay there, and lived within our means the remainder of my residency.

Our son, Stephen, was born during my second year of residency, and this little apartment was the only home he had known before we moved to Liberia.

We applied for the post-residency program of Samaritan's Purse in the spring of 2012 and were accepted that August.

In November, we met Dr. Rick Sacra, a medical missionary who had spent more than a decade and a half with his family in Liberia. Rick told me of his desire to start a family-medicine residency there for Liberian doctors. When I had looked ahead to working in missions, I had envisioned being able to train local physicians to care for their own people. I also wanted to teach them how to better follow Christ, while helping equip them to meet their people's physical and spiritual needs.

Rick's and my desires and our personalities seemed like a great match, so the following month Amber and I decided to accept a two-year term in Liberia. During that time, we hoped to figure out whether we would stay in Liberia permanently or if that would be our training ground for going somewhere else on our own.

LIFE IN LIBERIA

Amber

We moved to Liberia's capital city, Monrovia, in October 2013—Ruby now was four, and Stephen just six weeks shy of his third birthday.

Among the first missionaries we met were David and Nancy Writebol with Serving In Mission (SIM). Nancy was SIM's personnel coordinator. Because SIM managed ELWA Hospital, Nancy took responsibility for providing our orientation. She came to our home every day for the first couple of weeks to help our family adjust to living in a new country. Our kids started calling her Granny Nancy.

Nancy would take me into town and show me where I could go grocery shopping and how to get around the market areas. She also took me to what must have been every furniture store in Monrovia to help me find a couch and a dining-room table for our home.

She remained my shopping partner too. Going into town was expensive, because of gasoline prices, so the missionaries on the ELWA campus preferred to carpool into town or to take others' lists to save their having to make a trip.

Nancy was a youthful fifty-eight-year-old with blond hair and the relentless energy of a college student. On our shopping trips, we would zip into a store and if we didn't see what we were looking for right away, we would zip right back out and into another store, me pushing one of my kids in a cart and Nancy pushing the other. The carts' wheels, not to mention our feet, never stopped moving. I felt exhausted at the end of our shopping trips, but not Nancy.

The missionaries at ELWA lived in small homes and duplexes built along the beach. Kent and I have always thought we were fonder of mountains than beaches. I'd had little exposure to beaches and wondered if I would have to deal with sand in my hair all the time! But we loved where we lived.

We could step barefoot off our front porch and go for family walks along the beach after dinner. While Kent was working at the hospital—which could be long hours—I would take the kids out to climb on the rocks, collect seashells and sea glass, and find an occasional hermit crab we could adopt as a pet.

Living in Monrovia was not like living at home in the States where for recreational time we could take the kids to a park, a museum, the zoo, or a movie theater. But we found ways to improvise, like taking advantage of a hole in the water hose to convert it into a sprinkler, or filling a large basin with tap water and letting the kids use that as a swimming pool in the front yard.

Living there was very earthy.

Fresh fish was almost always available. We could watch from our porch as fishermen would leave early in the morning and then return late at night. They weren't the commercial fishermen we often see in the Western world. Some fished from a wooden boat with a sail and room enough for five or six workers. It was more common to see one person row out by himself in a dugout canoe with a net for catching fish. I don't know how they could row past the break, and it looked dangerous. At night we could see them coming back at the end of a long day, a tiny light shining from the LED lantern that gradually grew larger as the fisherman made it back to shore, on good days with enough fish to sell so he could provide for his family.

There was an entrepreneur named Edwin from whom I looked forward to buying fresh vegetables. In the tropical climate with dry winters and rainy summers, Liberia had several growing seasons, which allowed for gardening year round. Edwin would come around ELWA once a week, sometimes twice, with plastic bags filled with lettuce, Roma tomatoes, eggplants, and pineapples. One of the missionaries gave Edwin a wheelbarrow that enabled him to upgrade his delivery service.

Edwin's business was a real treat because it was rare to find fresh lettuce. Produce bought from the market had to be soaked in either bleach water or vinegar to kill the germs, and then we would have to rinse off each leaf with filtered water because the tap water wasn't safe to drink.

The pineapples in Liberia were incredibly delicious. There was no commercial pineapple industry, only individuals like Edwin who cut the tops off of pineapples and planted them to grow in their yards. We planted several in our yard, but we were told they take seven years to produce.

The Liberians are wonderful, beautiful people. On trips to market, I would try to talk to as many people as I could, asking their names and tribes, where they were from, and where they attended church. Because I was an American—a red-headed, light-skinned one at that—I stood out in the market, and people would remember me when they saw me.

Marion was my closest Liberian friend. She worked as our housekeeper during the day, cleaning and cooking us authentic Liberian meals. Marion taught me most of what I learned about Liberian culture. We also learned a lot from a friend named Praise, who was unofficially adopted by another missionary family on campus. Her four-year-old son, Theo, became our Stephen's best friend.

Our hearts just went out to the Liberians. The civil wars had left many people understandably distrustful, and it was against that obstacle that we tried to build relationships with them.

It was particularly difficult for Kent as a foreigner coming in to practice Western medicine, which sometimes went against the ways of local culture. That is why I viewed my top priorities as helping the kids grow up in a world that was new to us and maintaining a peaceful home for Kent to come to at the end of what could be long, tough days in the hospital and clinic.

EYE-OPENING INTRODUCTION

Kent

We had a few weeks to adjust to our new home before I began working in the hospital. My introduction to the challenge of being a doctor there came as quickly as my first patient.

Morris was a twelve-year-old boy with Type 1 diabetes. He had run out of insulin and didn't tell anyone in his family for a few days. By the time he came to our hospital, he had been vomiting for two or three days. He was dehydrated and very ill, with sky-high blood sugar. Morris had diabetic ketoacidosis (DKA), a potentially life-threatening complication caused by not taking insulin. We promptly began aggressive treatment with insulin and IV fluids.

I soon realized how treating Morris was different from my numerous DKA cases at John Peter Smith. First, there was no automatic pump on the IV fluids in ELWA Hospital. I had to calculate the fluid rate by the number of drips per minute coming from the plastic bottle of saline. The same went for the IV insulin infusion I had ordered. The medications were vital to Morris's survival, and we had to adjust them drip by drip, not giving him too much too quickly but also giving him enough to save his life.

Then I discovered what would be the most important difference in my treating diabetic patients there. During residency I had learned that it was not a patient's blood-sugar level that guides the treatment of DKA. Instead, the most important number came from the anion gap, a calculation derived from other laboratory values that included sodium, chloride, and carbon-dioxide levels. With Morris's life in my hands, I learned that our laboratory did not have the equipment needed to determine his pH level or his carbon-dioxide level. Without that information, I could not calculate his anion gap, basically leaving me flying blind with no equipment to tell me my altitude or airspeed.

We treated Morris to the best of our capabilities and prayed many times for him, but a few days later he passed away.

You can understand my disappointment: my first patient as a medical missionary was a twelve-year-old boy who died from a disease I thought I was fully capable of treating. Further, statistics told us that if he could have received adequate treatment, he would have had a 99 percent chance of surviving.

And so began my work in Liberia, among people still struggling to get to their feet after the wars, where death was a very real and present part of life even when—especially when—to me, it didn't seem it had to be.

There is simply no comparison between the medical resources available in Liberia and those available in the United States. To say it is apples and oranges would fall short of describing just how different the situations are. The Liberian doctors and nurses are skilled, compassionate people, but they are hindered by the lack of resources.

In the entire ELWA Hospital, which had forty-five to fifty beds, there were maybe four sinks with running water. At some of the sinks at night, it was necessary to wear a headlamp so we could see to properly scrub our hands.

The hospital was set up ward style, with up to eight patients in one big, open room. We had only four private rooms for patients.

There were none of the modern monitors for taking pulse and blood pressure, which seemed like minor inconveniences compared to the shortage of medications that often limited our treatment options.

Equipment taken for granted in the United States was unavailable or severely limited in Liberia. Consider a nasal cannula, for example. These are the small prongs inserted into a patient's nostrils to provide oxygen. I had a patient who was having trouble breathing, and I went to the nurse's station to ask for a nasal cannula so I could hook up the oxygen concentrator that would give the patient more oxygen for breathing.

"We don't have one," the nurse told me.

"What do you mean we don't have one?" I asked. "I just need a nasal cannula."

"We don't have any," she repeated.

I walked to the emergency room, where I was informed there was only one and it was already being used by a patient.

Then I went to the operating room, where there were only two that were reserved for emergency surgery.

There was not one extra nasal cannula available in the entire hospital. Back in the United States, these are single-use, disposable items because they are so readily available. I could go into an ICU room at a typical US hospital and probably find five sitting in a basket. We did not have that many in our entire hospital.

Every day we were forced to make decisions—and not just about nasal cannulas—that I never would have even needed to consider in an American hospital.

We also had a very limited range of drugs on the hospital formulary, and we often ran out of the drugs that we were supposed to have available. Some of that problem was cultural in origin.

Living a hand-to-mouth existence like many Liberians do—and perhaps the majority of the world does—there was little concept of setting things aside or storing up and saving to make sure there would be enough for the next day. The prevailing mind-set was to take what was there for now and then when it was gone, try to scrounge up more or make do with something else. It is difficult for anyone—anywhere, I suppose—to learn to work in a different manner from the way they live.

Money was another problem. Our drugs were supposed to come every six to nine months in a big shipment from Europe, and the budget was set up to pay at the time of those shipments. And that meant that we did not have the money to buy more drugs when we ran out.

Soon after Ebola hit, we ran out of gloves. Pre-Ebola we went through about nine boxes of gloves a day, but after we started treating patients with the disease, we used twenty boxes per day. Eventually the pharmacy had to ration gloves to the point that instead of having an empty box replaced with a new, full box, we would take our empty box to the pharmacy, where they would dispense five or ten pairs at a time.

Here is the irony: Liberia is one of the world's largest producers of raw latex, but all of its latex is exported. With no glove-making company there, rubber gloves have to be imported.

But we were short on more than just supplies. The wars had crippled the health-care infrastructure too. The people did not have appropriate access to basic health care. In a country of more than four million people, there were a total of fifty doctors. Add in the distrust of the government and the culture's way of dealing with the deceased, and Liberia was not prepared to confront Ebola.

PART 3

FIGHTING EBOLA

5

Life and Death

Kent

On Saturday, June 21, I toured Liberia's JFK Medical Center's reopened Ebola unit with Dr. Debbie and Dr. Tom Wood, an epidemiologist with Samaritan's Purse. We had been told JFK already had Ebola patients, but we learned that was not the case when we arrived. Instead, they were preparing to receive their first patient, with an ambulance en route.

JFK had set up a nice treatment unit, but they did not seem fully prepared. We had noticed some practical procedural steps that were not in place. How they would handle decontamination had not been determined. We did not see any wash stations or wash buckets between patients where the doctors and nurses could wash their hands. When we asked about the wash buckets, we were told they would be brought in when needed.

When dealing with a disease like Ebola, until those wash stations were in place, JFK was not ready. It was too risky to piece together safety precautions *after* a patient arrived. Every detail had to be mapped out and in place; otherwise the staff members would likely get infected.

I thought, *If they receive that patient right now, someone else is going to die.*

I could tell that Debbie and Tom were thinking along the same lines.

Following our tour, we were walking to our truck outside the hospital when an ambulance pulled up next to us. There were three people in the back with the Ebola patient.

"They are not ready," I said. "Their staff is going to get infected. More people will die if they receive that patient right now."

We wanted to be respectful and defer to the medical personnel at JFK, but they were not prepared for that Ebola patient. I called Dr. Nathaniel Varney, one of the leaders of the Ebola response for the Ministry of Health. He had given us the tour of the hospital's unit.

"Dr. Varney, your facility is great. Thank you for giving us a tour," I began. "We saw that the ambulance is here, and I just want to tell you that if there are any difficulties . . . I know you said you are ready, but it looked like there still are some things that need to happen before you receive a patient."

"Oh, no, no, no," Dr. Varney replied. "I'm not going to let them unload that patient from the ambulance until we have all of those things in place, like the wash buckets and other things. Don't worry. I am going to protect our staff."

"That's great," I told him. "But in case you hit some roadblocks putting those last details in place, I just want to extend an offer of help. If for whatever reason you cannot receive that patient right now, I want you to know that we are willing to help, and if that means you need to send that patient to ELWA, you can do that. And you could even send some of your staff to come help us, and we will teach them our process. We can do that together."

"Okay, thank you for that," he said. "I'll let you know if we have any problems."

We returned to our hospital, and that evening Jerry Brown received a phone call from the Ministry of Health saying they wanted to send an Ebola patient to us. I sat down with Dr. Brown in the midwife station outside the labor room, as he was taking phone calls regarding the patient. We talked between the calls.

"Jerry, who is this patient they want to send?" I asked. "If it is the patient that was arriving at JFK when we left, that is fine. Tell them to send some of their staff with them. That was the offer we made to them. But if they are able to receive that patient and they are saying they want to send a different one to us, no way. There is no sense whatsoever in sending one patient there and one patient here. Our unit is empty. If you send one patient here, we have to have a full staff for the unit for that one patient. We are going to pull people off shift in the hospital, and Debbie or I will have to stay up all night. If JFK can receive one patient, they can receive two, and it is better to put them together and not drain the resources of both facilities."

Dr. Brown soon learned that this was a different patient, a fourteen-year-old boy named Gebah who was related to someone high up within the Liberian government, who was specifically requesting the boy be treated at ELWA. Dr. Debbie volunteered to take the night shift and be there to receive Gebah when he arrived.

We were told the boy had tested positive and lived in Paynesville. That was a shock to us, because up to that point we had heard of positive Ebola tests only from New Kru Town. ELWA was located well to the southeast of Monrovia. We did learn that Gebah had not yet been tested and was from New Kru Town, not ELWA. With the pieces of the story not fitting together, we were suspicious.

The next morning I reported to work to relieve Dr. Debbie. She told me that the boy was fine. He had a little bit of fever, but no vomiting, no diarrhea, no rash; his eyes were not red, and he had reported no contact with anyone who'd had Ebola.

The uncle who brought him to the hospital had not been able to provide any further helpful information. As we dug into the boy's story more, we learned that the uncle who brought him was not the high-ranking government official. Gebah lived in New Kru Town, and the family's maid had been infected with Ebola. She started feeling ill while cooking at Gebah's house and got so sick that she could not leave to go home. She spent the night there and had a lot of diarrhea, and soon after, she died.

The high-ranking government official, also an uncle to the boy, was in the United States when he received a call that the maid had passed away. Through his connections, he had the maid's body tested and Gebah brought to his home in ELWA to get him out of New Kru Town.

A few days later, Gebah came down with a fever, but he continued going to school. For three or four days, he had fever and a headache that came and went. When his uncle found out, he had Gebah removed from his house and sent to our hospital. Gebah, who did not know the maid had Ebola, told us that they had been in the same house and used the same restroom.

We tested Gebah, and the result came back positive.

OUR SURVIVOR

I did not know how to tell Gebah he had Ebola. He was feeling well, with only a low-grade fever, and asking when he could leave the hospital. The first day I just told him that he would not be going home soon.

Each time we left the isolation unit, we went through our decontamination process on the back porch of the chapel we had converted into the treatment center. Gebah would step out onto another area of the porch, sit in a chair, and watch us. On the second day after Gebah's test had come back positive, I sat down on the porch near him.

"Gebah, we are friends, right?" I asked him.

"Yeah."

"I want you to know that you can trust me," I continued. "I want you to know that we are here to take care of you. We want to do what's best for you. Because you are my friend, I need to tell you something. You know that Ebola Virus Disease that is going around? We tested you for it, and the test says you have that virus. Some people can die from that virus, but you are so strong and you are looking so good and doing so well. We are going to pray to God that you beat this virus, and we are going to help you every way we can. We will continue to take good care of you and pray for you, but because I am your friend, I needed to tell you that."

Gebah took the news very well, probably because he did not feel like he was carrying a deadly virus.

Gebah's sister came to the hospital every day to check on his condition and drop off his favorite foods for us to give him. I talked to her to make sure the Ministry of Health had been in contact with her family, had told her about the positive test result, and had explained how the family members needed to evaluate themselves for fevers.

Some of our nurses positioned themselves outside the door of the isolation unit and read Bible stories to Gebah as he sat just inside the door and listened attentively. We gave him a notepad and a pencil, and Gebah would write and draw all sorts of pictures. Anything we gave him that had words on it, he copied into his notepad. His mind needed to be active while he was in our unit.

Although he continued to feel well, he watched the suffering of other Ebola patients in our unit that no fourteen-year-old boy should have to witness. The Ebola patients that came in after him died miserable, horrible, graphic deaths, sometimes only six feet away from Gebah. It scared him. He never told us that, but we could tell. When a patient died and we decontaminated the body and prepared it for burial, Gebah would leave the room to sit outside.

One night there was a patient in total misery. We were doing everything we could for her, but she was rolling back and forth in her bed, moaning and crying loudly. Gebah did not sleep that night. He sat in a chair next to the door, wanting someone to talk to him or to read to him all night long.

The next day, I asked Gebah, "What do you want? Is there something I can bring you?"

He wanted a soccer ball. I asked Amber if she could get one for him. Our kids had one, and she brought it over as I was leaving shift. Then I gave the ball to one of the nurses to give to Gebah that night.

After my next shift, our team was exiting the unit to decontaminate. That was about a fifteen-minute process, and as the team leader I would be the last to leave. Gebah followed his routine of stepping out on the porch to watch us, and while I was waiting my turn, I asked Gebah if he wanted to kick the soccer ball around in the yard.

He nodded with a big smile.

In full PPE, I kicked the ball with Gebah, and we juggled it a little bit to compare our skills.

Gebah's fever went away on his sixth day in the isolation unit, and after three days of no fever, we ran another test for Ebola. It came back negative. We began preparing for Gebah to leave us.

We soaked all his clothes in bleach, which ruined them. We had him take a bucket bath with bleach water and soap, and then rinsed him off with fresh water. We wrapped him in a clean towel and had him walk through our decontamination area, just as he had watched us do, and sprayed his feet with bleach. Then he stepped into a clean area and put on a soccer jersey, shorts, and new flip-flops his family had brought him.

Amber had gone to the market and bought Gebah a toothbrush, soap, deodorant, and a new pair of shoes. Ruby and Stephen had added coloring books and toy trucks of theirs that they had picked out for him from home. Amber gave these goodies to Gebah in a mesh sports bag.

We explained to Gebah's family how he was no longer contagious, but that they still had to continue monitoring themselves through the end of their twenty-one-day incubation period. Gebah posed for photos with some of us who had treated him, and then he left, fully healthy.

Gebah would be our only Ebola patient to walk out of our chapel isolation unit. All the others died.

CUSTOMS CHALLENGES

Early during Gebah's stay, I was called to the ER when a deceased patient showed up in a taxi cab. In a country with no emergency-response service, taxis were the most common means of transportation to the hospital.

If a nurse thought a patient arriving by taxi appeared to be dead, regardless of the cause, standard procedure was to call a doctor to come see the person in the taxi instead of removing the body from the cab. We would evaluate the patient there because the family members typically preferred to take the body back home with them, so this way there was no need to remove the body, only to return it to the cab.

I received one of those calls regarding a taxi that came in from Jacob Town. I exited the front door of the ER to the yellow, four-door, compact sedan. The patient, a young, slender, well-dressed woman named Rita, was in the middle of the backseat, fully dressed, head leaning back slightly. She was sitting completely still, and I could tell from a distance that she was either not breathing or not breathing deeply.

Two family members were with her, and the taxi driver and a small crowd of people stood around the car. The woman had been sitting between her husband and her brother in the back seat. Her brother was the responsible family member, and I asked him what had happened. He informed me that his sister had been sick for a few days with a fever and also had developed diarrhea. On the way to the hospital, she had experienced difficulty breathing.

I was wearing a plastic apron over my scrubs and two pairs of gloves on my hands. I carefully leaned into the cab, touching as little of the back seat as possible. I could tell she was dead. I inserted the tip of a thermometer into her ear, and her temperature was 103.8. I felt her neck to confirm she had no pulse.

I backed out of the cab and put one gloved hand over the thermometer and pulled the glove off so that the thermometer was completely covered. I took my other glove off without touching the outside of it.

Prince, the hospital janitor, came walking past, and I asked him to bring a sprayer out to the cab. I placed the thermometer on the sidewalk and had Prince decontaminate it. Then he sprayed my hands and the rest of me from the neck down, all over the plastic apron and even my shoes. I began talking to the family, explaining that I suspected the woman had died of Ebola—and what that meant for those who may have been exposed. I told them that we needed to keep her body at the hospital until we could receive the result of an Ebola test. If she was confirmed to have the virus, the Ministry of Health burial team would help bury her body in a safe manner.

My plan seemed straightforward to me and clearly the safe procedure to follow. But in Liberian culture, it is not acceptable to leave the dead body of a family member at the hospital. Common practice following a death was to take the body home and lay it out where close family members would bathe the body. Then community members came to the home to grieve, with people lying across the body and kissing their deceased loved one. A lot of touching of the body took place, and often the body was buried within twenty-four hours of death. A person with Ebola is most contagious at time of death, and a dead body remains contagious for days.

The brother seemed to understand the importance of what I was saying, but he could not give me permission to keep the body because the body belonged to the husband. The husband was dealing with the grief of losing his wife, whom he had not wanted to believe was dead until after I had examined her in the cab. In addition, the husband had just been told that his wife might have had Ebola, and that meant he had been exposed to the disease. He was not in a good frame of mind to be thinking about the bigger picture.

"Please don't take her body away. Please don't do this," I begged the husband. "For your own safety, for your own good, don't take her body. Please. We will treat her well. We will take care of her body, put her into a morgue, and if she does not have Ebola, you can come back and take her and bury her the way you want. But if she has Ebola, it could cost you your life to take her now."

Dr. Afidu Lemfuka, a missionary doctor from the Democratic Republic of Congo, had been working in the clinic that day. He was headed back to the ER when he came near us. I called out to him. "Dr. Lemfuka, I need your help right now," I told him. "Please get suited up."

The husband, however, was not willing to wait any longer.

"No, no, we are going," he said, then ordered the driver to get back into the taxi and to leave with the body still inside.

In one of my most desperate moments while I was in West Africa, I got down on the ground and held on to the husband's ankle. In Liberia, there is a saying: "I hold your foot." It is a figurative way of saying "I am begging you." In this case, I was on the ground, literally holding on to the man's foot, begging him not to leave with his wife's body.

I called over a security guard and asked him to request his commander come there right away. New cases were being reported at a quickening rate, and I knew that if this lady's body was taken home, the outbreak would never end. The family's lives were at risk. My life was at risk. If they took her home and the community came to mourn her death and touched her, the lives of people throughout Monrovia were at risk.

Mr. John Vokpo, the security commander, arrived just in time.

"There is no security issue here," I told him. "I am not asking you to arrest anyone. But I desperately need your help."

I quickly explained the situation and asked if he could talk to the husband and brother about leaving the body with us. Mr. Vokpo took the two aside, listened to their perspective, and pleaded with them to cooperate for their own well-being and the well-being of the community.

The discussion went on for about half an hour, with the crowd growing larger.

A mentally challenged man named Peter hung around our hospital. Sometimes he would come to the clinic as a patient, but most of the time he was there to beg for food or a little money. He came near the cab, so I shouted, "Peter, get away from here! Go away and do not come over here anymore!"

I feared Peter would die because these people had come to the hospital with a possible Ebola patient and refused to leave without taking the body, and Peter would not know to avoid contact with them.

Finally, the efforts of Mr. Vokpo paid off, and the husband gave consent for us to keep her body so we could administer an Ebola test.

Dr. Lemfuka came out in his protective gear, and I rushed inside to put on mine. We took a stretcher and a spray can of bleach to the car. We sprayed Rita's body in the back seat, and I asked the driver if he wanted the inside of his taxi sprayed. He did.

Then we took her body out of the taxi and laid her on the stretcher. We covered her face with a cloth and sprayed her body again before covering her with a sheet. Dr. Lemfuka and I picked up the stretcher and carried her into the triage tent. I uncovered the body and opened her blouse so I could take a blood sample directly from her heart. When a person dies, the blood begins to clot and the body has no blood pressure. With no pulse, it is difficult to find a vein to draw from. The heart chamber, however, is full of blood, so we take blood from there.

I had a long, 18-gauge spinal needle to go through her chest wall and into her heart. The chest wall was hard, and I bent three needles trying to draw the sample. As I prepared the fourth, I was told that it was our last one.

"Okay, let's pray," I said. "God, help me. Please help me. Protect us and keep us safe. Please help me get this. Help this needle to work. Just help."

I was able to penetrate through to the heart and draw a 4 cc blood sample. The next day, the test came back positive.

~

A few days later, a two-and-a-half-year-old girl named Aletha was brought to us after five days of fever.

"Where has this girl been?" I asked her mother.

"Jacob Town," the mother answered.

Rita had come from Jacob Town.

"Do you know Rita?" I asked the mother.

The little girl was Rita's sister-in-law.

Fortunately, it turned out that Aletha did not have Ebola. Still, it was a heart-wrenching connection for me to know that not only had Rita died from Ebola, but now we were also treating her two-and-a-half-year-old sister-in-law. But I did wonder if other family members were sick and not coming to the hospital because they were angry about our keeping the body?

On days like that, I would leave the hospital feeling defeated, because not only were we fighting against Ebola, but also the cultural customs that worked against our efforts to stop the outbreak.

6

"Love Your Neighbor as Yourself"

Kent

Compassion was a core motivation for my becoming a doctor and a missionary. It was for the sake of showing compassion to people in need that I went to medical school. And it was compassion for people that led our family to Liberia.

The English word *compassion* derives from the Latin *compati,* "to suffer with." It means to come alongside others in such a way that you actually share in their suffering.

Choosing to have compassion means opening yourself up to take on hurt that belongs to someone else—you choose to enter into that person's pain and share the burden.

Two of the more heartbreaking cases of Ebola came to our hospital on June 28. Lusu was a tall woman of moderate build, in her mid- to late-fifties. She was stoic. When I looked at Lusu, I could tell she had lived a difficult life. She was a proud woman who appeared to have always been a hard worker. Her arms and legs were strong; she was not an idle woman.

Josephine, her daughter, was about thirty. She was not as tall as her mother, and her face was a little rounder. Although her skin was dark, it was not as dark as her mother's, but her build was similar to Lusu's.

Lusu's other daughter, Princess, was a nurse. Princess had contracted Ebola while treating a patient at a different hospital. Lusu and Josephine had cared for her until her death, and a few days later they both began showing symptoms of the disease.

On July 2–3 I worked a 24-hour shift, from 6 p.m. to 6 p.m. that Wednesday through Thursday. Early Thursday morning, shortly after 1 a.m., we were outside the unit when Josephine suddenly cried out, moaning as loudly as her body would allow. We shouted through the door that we would come inside to check on her as soon as we could.

It would take us fifteen minutes to suit up, and we wanted to hurry to help Josephine yet could not rush too much and put ourselves at risk. While we were suiting up, the room went silent. I looked through the window and saw that Josephine was lifeless, laid back sideways across the edge of her bed, arms splayed out.

Generally, we did not go immediately into the unit to take care of a dead body. We allowed time—depending on the circumstances, sometimes a few hours—for the virus to disperse. But Lusu's bed sat at the foot of Josephine's bed. Lusu had already watched her other daughter die from Ebola, and she had a sister isolated in a treatment center at another hospital. Now Josephine had just passed away in front of her.

As team leader, it was my decision to enter the unit to take care of Josephine's body. I instructed two team members to string a rope from the ceiling between Lusu's and Josephine's beds and hang a temporary curtain to shield Lusu from Wilton, one of the nurses, and me as we prepared Josephine's body for the morgue.

After Wilton and I verified that Josephine was deceased, we gathered a sprayer and supplies for wrapping the body. We also put on heavy-duty rubber gloves over our two pairs of surgical gloves. Because we would not need the tactile ability required in treating live patients, we could wear the rubber gloves as an extra layer of protection.

We sprayed Josephine and the bed around her multiple times. Because she apparently had been sitting up and fell back across the bed, we had to turn her lengthwise on the bed. I remember thinking as I grabbed her head and shoulders, *This is the most dangerous thing I have ever done in my life.* I was completely confident in our protective gear, but there is nothing more dangerous than handling the body of an Ebola victim who has just died. However, there was no way I would allow Josephine's lifeless body to remain mere feet from her mother.

A curious trend I observed with Ebola patients is that rigor mortis develops rapidly. I had observed this the night we received our first Ebola patient when I removed the backpack from beneath Felicia's uncle, and I had noted it in patients since. There may be many causes of death that lead to quick rigor mortis, but it seemed odd to me. Fast onset of rigor mortis was another layer of eeriness with Ebola.

With Josephine's body, it was difficult to bring in her arms and straighten out her legs. Her arms kept wanting to go back to the position they were in at the moment she had died. In the end, we had to tie her wrists together to wrap her body for burial.

After we decontaminated Josephine's body with the bleach solution, we wrapped her in four layers of plastic, spraying each layer separately. Then we put the body on a rubberized, waterproof mattress cover and overlapped the edges, rolled them down, and tied them with a strip of cloth. Then we carried the body to our temporary morgue, which was a UNICEF tent in the courtyard outside the isolation unit but still within the high-risk zone.

The Ministry of Health had a burial team of men wearing full PPE who would come and collect the bodies of Ebola victims. At that stage of the outbreak, the burial team would load a body onto a truck and bury it where the family wished. The family was allowed to have a memorial service at the burial, but the team members were the only people who handled the body. Later, as the deaths increased to an overwhelming number, that procedure had to change. The Ministry of Health had to resort to putting bodies in mass graves and, eventually, began cremations, which created controversy because that violated some Liberian religious beliefs and practices.

Unfortunately, because of how rapidly the deaths were mounting, it took more than sixty hours for the Ministry of Health to come and take Josephine from our morgue. In fact, Dr. Brown refused to take in any more suspected Ebola patients until the burial team came to pick up Josephine and other bodies that were waiting.

The day after Josephine died, I checked on Lusu. She had been very sick, with a lot of diarrhea. Lusu had been quiet and withdrawn in the unit, and I could not imagine what she was going through. Two daughters had died from Ebola, her sister was presumably dying at another hospital, and with her own health deteriorating, she had to feel her time was not far away.

"Can I sing a song to you?" I asked her.

She nodded.

I started in on a song from our staff devotionals. Every time I sang it, I felt overwhelmed.

No matter what I face,
I will praise You, Lord.
When troubles come my way,
I will praise You, Lord.

Today O, I will lift up my voice in praise.
For I know that, You are always there for me.
Almighty God, You're my all in all.
No matter what I face,
When troubles come my way,
I will praise You, Lord![2]

I had marveled at hearing Liberians sing that song at the top of their lungs, with full recognition of its meaning as they concluded with "When troubles come my way, I will praise You, Lord!" As they sang, I tried to imagine all the suffering they had endured, with the civil wars, the tumultuous years preceding the conflicts, and then the difficulties that had followed.

I finished the song. Lusu looked me in the eyes, squeezed my hand, and gave me an affirming nod.

A couple of days after Josephine's death, Lusu began to open up more with us. One nurse in particular, Kelly, sat next to Lusu's bed, and Lusu just talked and talked to her and then asked, "Will you pray with me?"

Kelly wrote a blog post about what she considered a profound moment of making that personal connection with this lady who had been there for eight days and appeared near death. As doctors and nurses, we can become so wrapped up in our duties that, unfortunately, we forget the decencies we typically would have with people. Lusu taught us a lesson in that.

I was in the unit one time when Lusu had diarrhea. The nurse cared for Lusu, cleaned up the mess, then washed her hands. Lusu, though, was not able to see the nurse washing up because I was standing in her line of sight.

When the nurse returned to give Lusu food, Lusu became indignant. It was difficult to understand Lusu sometimes, but she was obviously telling us to get away from her and go wash our hands. She was not going to let anyone touch her feces and then try to feed her. Lusu held tight to her dignity even though Ebola was trying to steal it away from her.

We apologized profusely and explained that the nurse had washed her hands. "We would never do that to you," we told her. The nurse returned to the wash station and rewashed her hands so that Lusu could see her.

We were giving our patients the best care we could, but we learned from Lusu the importance of letting them see that we were. It is easy for caregivers to forget because of the nature of our jobs, but Lusu was a great example that despite everything the disease was doing to her, she was still a person and wanted to be treated as one.

There is a phenomenon in Ebola called pseudoremission, where a patient can drastically improve for up to forty-eight hours before the bottom falls out on their condition and they die. I do not know the physiology behind pseudoremission, but it is why we require Ebola patients to be well for at least three days before we test to see if they are negative for the virus.

Like Felicia, our first Ebola patient, Lusu experienced pseudoremission. After being so sick at the time of Josephine's death, Lusu's condition improved for two days. We all were hopeful that she would become our second survivor. She had those two days of really opening up and being more outgoing and interactive with us, then she crashed over a twenty-four-hour period and died on July 7, four days after her daughter.

INCOMPLETE HISTORIES

The day that Lusu died, we received another patient who presented a common challenge we faced in preventing the spread of the disease.

Harris was a plumber, thirty-one years of age. Dr. Fankhauser evaluated Harris and placed him in the triage tent in order to separate him from other patients while he put together a more thorough medical history of Harris.

Harris's family brought him to the hospital after he had been sick for a few days. The family was worried about Harris, but they would not say what specifically they were worried about. They would not say they feared he had Ebola.

John regarded Harris as very open in describing his history. Harris said he lived in Mombo Town, near the hot spot of New Kru Town, and although he was aware of the Ebola outbreak nearby, he claimed not to know anyone who had been sick with or died from Ebola. Unable to identify possible contact with anyone who'd had Ebola, John left Harris in the triage tent so that he would not be exposed to the virus in the isolation unit. However, John remained suspicious and had blood drawn from Harris for an Ebola test.

While Harris was in triage, he began vomiting and having diarrhea, and his eyes began turning red. All are classic symptoms of Ebola.

When I came on shift that night, I walked into the tent to obtain more history from Harris. In Liberia, the first history is rarely the full history: it is difficult for Liberians to communicate with a foreigner, and they also are hesitant to open up. Liberians have this sense that if they speak something negative, it might come true. And if they do not speak something negative, it will not happen. They believe that if they said "I think I might have Ebola" or "I think I might die," then that could cause them to get the disease or to die.

Harris told me, as he had told John, that he was a plumber.

"In your work as a plumber," I asked, "do you ever come in contact with people's runny stomach?" That was how Liberians sometimes referred to diarrhea.

When he answered that he did, my suspicion increased. I thought he might have unknowingly been exposed to Ebola. With his worsening condition, I decided to transfer Harris into the treatment unit so we would not have to split the staff between the unit and the triage tent.

The next morning, Harris told me that after all, he did know of someone who had died from Ebola. He said the man had sold slippers in the Duala Market. Both Mombo Town and New Kru Town are part of Duala. But Harris said he did not know the man.

That day, Harris's test came back positive for Ebola.

Another characteristic of Liberian culture is that families do not always want the patient to know his diagnosis out of fear that if the patient learns he has an incurable disease, he might fall over dead or give up hope and die in short time. Again, *speak negative and negative could happen.*

Hiding a diagnosis goes completely against the mind-set of Western medical culture. I believed I needed to tell Harris about his test result, and I worried about how he might take the news. He was a strong, strapping guy, and I did not know if he would get upset and start thrashing around the treatment unit, or try to run away, or who knows what else.

I did not tell him that he had Ebola, choosing to speak in vague terms instead.

"You know, Harris, you are going to be here for a while. We are going to keep taking care of you the best we can."

I intentionally did not mention the word *Ebola.* The next time I went into the unit, a few hours later, I sat on his bed and told him as gently as I could that his test had come back positive, that he did indeed have Ebola.

We typically went into the unit three times during a normal shift, and my next time in, Harris said he wanted to talk.

"I was thinking about it," Harris told me, "and I remember the guy's name, that slippers salesman."

Harris gave me his name and said, "He was sick at his house and started vomiting blood. Everybody ran away, and his wife wanted to take him to the hospital. She called a taxi, so I went over and I helped pick him up and carry him to the taxi. The taxi started going to the hospital and the guy died, so the taxi turned around and brought his body home. They unloaded his body at home."

Because a community leader had called the Ministry of Health to report the mysterious death, the next day a team from the ministry came to collect the body and decontaminate. Harris saw the team members in their "space suits" and went over to talk to them. The workers told Harris that the guy probably had cholera and that he should be careful. Harris gave the team his name and phone number so he could be called if needed.

The dead man's wife ran away, scared, and Harris never heard anything more about the man or his test result. Six days later, Harris began feeling ill. He was being a good Samaritan and had contracted Ebola as a result. Five days after he came to ELWA, Harris died. He was two years younger than I.

SAYING YES

When I reflect on patients like Lusu, Josephine, and Harris, I do not feel like a failure—that my caregiving was somehow lacking. Even though they died, I feel that I did something more for them than simply treat their sickness. I did everything I could to save their lives to no avail, but I also had compassion on them. I entered into their suffering with them. I tried to offer back to them the dignity that Ebola was taking away. It is a humiliating disease. It puts its victims in a totally hopeless situation.

Once a patient enters the isolation unit as a suspected case, she has no contact with another human being. Any person who touches her does so through two pairs of surgical gloves, and that touch is from a person whose face she cannot see. All that our patients could see of us was our eyes through our protective goggles. It is a dehumanizing way for life to end.

For my patients, they could see through my goggles that I was white, so I was a foreigner, a stranger to them. That can be difficult for patients—to be cared for by people they do not know. I encourage people who hear my stories to try to put themselves into that situation and see how they would feel. As doctors and nurses, we tried to do just that.

We were conscientious about introducing ourselves by name when we entered the isolation unit. We wrote our names with a Sharpie across the chest of our PPE or across our forehead to help those who could read. We wrote our names on our backs as well, to help identify us when facing away from patients.

We called patients by name. We had conversations with them beyond just their medical conditions. We did everything we could to try to give Ebola patients their humanity back.

The day I sat next to Lusu's bed and sang to her, I held her hand while wearing two pairs of gloves. Because I knew and trusted the protocols, I never shied away from touching patients.

∽

During my residency at JPS, Dr. David and Joan McRay hosted a small group of residents every Tuesday for dinner and a discussion about life, faith, and medicine. One of the recurring topics of conversation was the idea of saying yes to people— being fully present, opening our lives to people, and, upon invitation, entering into their lives in a meaningful way.

It is impossible to respond with this existential yes to every person we encounter. No person has the time or emotional energy to enter every encounter in this way. We must acknowledge that saying yes to everyone is simply not possible. The question then becomes, to whom do I say yes today? To whom am I going to open up and enter into that person's circumstances on a deeper level—beyond the superficial?

That was an ongoing conversation on those Tuesday nights, because those are difficult questions to answer. The discussions influenced me as I meditated more deeply on the actions of Jesus in my favorite Bible verse: "When Jesus landed and saw a large crowd, he had compassion on them, because they were like sheep without a shepherd."[3]

What did it look like now to have compassion on people in need—especially in my role as physician and missionary? I could not say yes to every patient. In Liberia, because of those discussions at the McRays' home, I was conscious of the times I said yes, as well as the times when I did not.

Tension sometimes exists between the roles of physician and missionary. I wrestle with this tension as I consider my primary identity. Am I primarily a Christ follower who is a physician, or is my first identity found in my occupation? But the way I see it, the difference is not so great. As a follower of Jesus, I am called to have compassion and mercy on people. Not only on Christian people. Not only on non-Christians. Not only on Americans. Not only on foreigners. Not only on people who can pay back whatever they owe me. I am to show compassion and mercy to everyone. This is my task as a follower of Jesus. Likewise, physicians are expected to render care to anyone and everyone. Period.

But the doctor-patient relationship is not one of equality. It involves a power differential. And just like any other relationship, the one in the position of power must respect the vulnerability of the one seeking help. It is wrong for a doctor to use the position of power over a patient to impose religious teachings on someone who may not feel like he has any choice but to listen and agree. I do not sit at the bedside of every sick patient and preach at him.

But articulating the motivation for my service and my sense of compassion is part of saying yes, of inviting the person in front of me to enter into my life in a deeper way. And my motivation for who I am and what I do centers on the love and the mercy and the grace and the compassion of Jesus Christ.

If the circumstances arise where a patient wants to know about those motivations, then I may have an opportunity to share. But I try to be diligent not to use my position in the doctor-patient relationship to coerce a patient either to hear my message or to agree with my beliefs.

There are people who have serious grumbles against medical missions, because they think its purpose is to leverage that power in patients' moments of vulnerability to coerce them into embracing a particular religion. But there is nothing coercive about Jesus.

Jesus healed many people who did not follow him. I believe I am called to do the same. His healing was not predicated on their acceptance of his message. Jesus healed because he had compassion on people. And I seek to have that same kind of compassion on my patients.

Jesus once was asked which of the commandments was most important. He answered, "Love the Lord your God with all your heart and with all your soul and with all your mind and with all your strength." Then he added, unsolicited, these words: "The second is this: 'Love your neighbor as yourself.'"[4]

It is human nature to be concerned about the well-being of people we know. But when we reach the point where we have that same sense of concern and compassion for people we do not know, who are facing some sort of difficulty, trial, or danger, I believe that is what Jesus is talking about when he said to love our neighbors as ourselves.

I do not have it within me to create that sense of compassion on my own. I cannot say yes to everyone every day. But when I recognize not only the mercy that God has had on me but also the profound depth of that mercy, his mercy will overflow in my life and extend to the people around me. It is not my compassion but the compassion that Jesus has had on me that I extend to other people.

I said yes to Lusu, to Gebah, to Harris, and to other patients. But there were other patients to whom I gave the same level of medical care and the same humanity and dignity, but to whom I was not able to say yes.

When I was sitting beside Lusu's bed holding her hand, I was not holding the hands of those other patients. It is impossible to hold every patient's hand at the same time. I cannot explain how I made the decisions of whom to say yes to. Sometimes, it was a matter of circumstance. Sometimes, it was by choice.

This much I do know: if we all say yes to someone, then everyone will be taken care of.

7

An Overwhelming Challenge

Amber

By mid-July, Kent's schedule felt to me like his intern year all over again. Perhaps worse. His hours were insane. Most days Kent worked sixteen to eighteen hours. It wasn't uncommon for him to go to work at 7 a.m. and not come home until noon the following day. He would sleep an hour and a half or so, wake up to phone calls from the hospital, drink a cup of coffee, and return to work that evening. I didn't know how Kent could keep working at that pace without making himself sick.

Lord, help him, I would pray.

Sometimes too busy to eat a meal, Kent had lost more than 30 pounds since we moved to Liberia, dropping from 198 pounds to 165. The other doctors and nurses were under the same physical and emotional stress as Kent.

As the outbreak reached the point of explosion, the missionary community rallied together. Some of us who were full-time mothers took on the task of washing the treatment unit's laundry, and with additional medical personnel and volunteers answering calls for help, the laundry was endless.

The doctors and nurses wore scrubs under their PPE. Because of the humidity and the lack of air conditioning in the buildings, the temperature underneath the suits could reach 115 degrees. They could wear the scrubs for only a few hours before they had to change because of all the sweat.

Worried about Kent skipping meals, I liked to take him something to eat. And if I was taking food for Kent, I decided I might as well take food and snacks for the others working at the hospital. They needed to eat and drink water regularly. They already were missing out on sleep, and if they did not get the food and water they needed, they were setting themselves up for getting sick at a time when every staff person in the hospital was needed.

Someone would bake a big pan of cinnamon rolls for the night crew as a way to encourage them. Someone else would take banana bread or another dessert a different night. Supporting the hospital workers became a unifying team effort.

We especially wanted to take care of the volunteers who had come to ELWA through Samaritan's Purse. They were responding to a crisis, and a dangerous one at that. We wanted to be as welcoming to them as we could.

With Ebola no longer limited to certain geographical areas, life in Liberia changed. The spread of the disease heightened the underlying tension and distrust of government. All around Monrovia, people were nervous about being in crowds. At market you would have no idea if the other people there were well or not, or if they'd had any contact with Ebola victims.

In the city there was limited access to clean water, so many people could not practice proper hygiene.

Churches became a spreading ground for Ebola. A sick person would go to church to be prayed for, and other believers would crowd around him, laying hands on him and praying. A local healer contracted Ebola while praying for a couple of Ebola victims, and she later got ill and died.

Kent spoke in our church one Sunday to inform the people about Ebola. He told them what they could do to protect themselves, such as not going to the marketplace and not shaking hands with people. There was a designated time in our services when we would walk around during a song and greet each other by shaking hands. The pastor told the congregation that because of the Ebola virus, it would be okay for those not comfortable shaking hands to simply wave to others in the church. But a man in the front row of the congregation openly disapproved.

"I don't agree with that," he spoke up. "We are brothers and sisters. It is our tradition. We have no fear. We have the Lord." So, following tradition, we sang and greeted everyone, shaking anyone's hand that was offered.

We already had made a habit of taking our own hand sanitizer to church and discreetly using it. As adults, Kent and I knew how to be safe, but out of concern for our children, we stopped going into town for church. Instead, we started meeting with our neighbors in their homes on campus, streaming YouTube videos for our praise and worship time.

At home we stocked up on cans of powdered milk, dried noodles, beans, and frozen chicken. We didn't know how bad the outbreak would become, but we made preparations so that we could remain inside our home for a few months if necessary.

COMING TOGETHER

Kent

A few years earlier, Franklin Graham, president and CEO of Samaritan's Purse, had held a festival in Liberia. When he saw how aged the ELWA Hospital had become, he committed SP to funding and constructing a new hospital on the campus for SIM to manage. That was in the works when we moved to Monrovia, with December 2014 planned as a completion date.

The cinder-block chapel we had converted into a temporary isolation unit during the spring had room for only five beds and storage, and it was obvious that it was on the verge of becoming undersized. We did not know how soon we would need more beds for Ebola patients, but it would not be long. So we chose the kitchen and laundry building of the new hospital as the best site for the new unit. Construction of the new hospital was halted in order to complete the larger unit that would allow us to treat more Ebola patients.

I had been appointed medical director of the new unit, which would be called ELWA 2, with the chapel becoming known as ELWA 1. The decision had been made to consolidate all the Ebola patients to one location, so ELWA 1 and JFK would become one facility—ELWA 2—and in preparation, I began tracking how many Ebola patients were in our county.

Up until about mid-July, we were treating one to three patients on a typical day at our hospital. On July 16, there were two patients at ELWA 1 and two at JFK, either confirmed or suspected. On July 20, the day we moved into ELWA 2, there were thirteen patients. Over the next two days, eight more patients came in. In less than a week, we had gone from four to more than twenty. As some patients were dying and some were being discharged when their tests came back negative, all available beds were not empty for long.

It was intense dealing with a horrific, scary disease as we saw more and more deaths.

I had learned to deal with death during residency. Only one patient I had treated in clinic in residency wound up dying after being admitted to the hospital. But I dealt with patients, including trauma patients, who came in and soon died, or were critically ill and admitted into the intensive care unit. I had led conversations with families about a loved one with a poor prognosis, or shared the news that their loved one had passed away. I had worked side by side with the reality of death and not been overwhelmed by it. That is one of the strange things about working in the medical field: life and death coexist on a daily basis. I would have to sit down with a family to tell them that their loved one had just died, then fifteen minutes later my clinic shift would be starting and I'd have to grab a bite to eat on the way. That's our job.

Despite that training, the number of deaths in Liberia became overwhelming for me, far exceeding anything I had experienced in the United States.

And that was before Ebola.

It was not uncommon for me to sign three or four death certificates in a twenty-four-hour period. The deceased could be a seventy-eight-year-old who'd had a stroke, a fifty-year-old with cancer, a twenty-four-year-old with HIV, and in another case an eighteen-month-old whose mother stuffed food in his mouth because he was sick and hadn't eaten for two days, resulting in the boy choking, aspirating the food, and dying.

That was difficult enough to deal with, and then in the first seven weeks of treating Ebola patients, our patients had a 5 percent survival rate.

Our jobs were physically and emotionally draining. We had to process on our own, out loud, and as part of a team. I knew it had to be even harder on Nancy Writebol, SIM's personnel coordinator. She had previously become a certified nursing assistant but had not worked in a health-care setting, and as we had prepared for a potential outbreak, she had volunteered to serve as a hygienist in our unit.

The hygienist in an ETU could be expected to cover a wide range of duties, depending on how many people staffed a unit. In an understaffed unit like ours, a hygienist could help doctors and nurses dress and undress, decontaminate, wash boots and goggles, serve as a runner, and handle the unit's inventory.

Among her duties Nancy took on the critical assignment of mixing the bleach solution. She became affectionately known as the Bleach Lady. Hers was a support job, but it was one of the most important responsibilities in the hospital, because that person had to be someone the health-care providers could fully trust to be detail oriented and meticulous.

A new bleach solution had to be prepared every twenty-four hours, and the mix had to be just right. Too much bleach and the solution could be harmful to skin and internally if breathed in. Too little bleach and it might not kill the pathogens that needed to be killed, and that would present major contamination risks.

As part of helping us suit up, the hygienist put tape over certain pieces of gear to prevent our skin from being exposed. Body fluids could potentially splash beneath loose gear and come into contact with skin.

With our gloves, for example, we would pull the sleeves of the PPE down over the first pair of gloves and the hygienist would wrap tape tightly around the wrists. Then we would put on a second pair of gloves and pull the glove cuffs over the sleeve, with the hygienist adding a second layer of tape. The first taped glove kept our sleeves from pulling loose, and the second prevented the glove from sliding down and fluid getting inside the glove.

Nancy felt the weight of the responsibility implicit in her job, and when she would tape my gloves, she would tape one arm and say, "This is for Stephen," and tape the other and say, "and this one is for Ruby."

The doctors and nurses put their lives in the hands of the hygienists, and Nancy had our complete trust.

Nancy and I had numerous conversations about what was going on around us. The experience built a bond among all of us in the unit, but Nancy and I especially began developing a deeper relationship. In fact, she had begun calling me her son, and she felt like a mother to me.

REST AND HELP ON THE WAY

I'd had two consecutive days off (mostly) the weekend of July 5–6, allowing me to tackle the overdue tasks at home of repairing the refrigerator door, unclogging the kitchen drain, fixing a drawer in Ruby's room, and replacing the training wheels on Stephen's bicycle.

I also had two weeks of vacation coming and was looking forward to that as a time of rest and recovery. Amber's brother, Keith, was getting married in early August in Abilene. Amber, Ruby, and Stephen would go ahead of me, and I would fly out about a week later. My parents and my sister Krista were going to come down from Indianapolis to see us, and then on August 10, Amber, the kids, and I would fly back to Liberia accompanied by my dad, who would work with us temporarily in the hospital.

My parents had planned on visiting us in Monrovia for Thanksgiving and staying for four or five weeks, with my dad helping at the hospital. A few weeks earlier, my parents and my dad's cousin and her husband had been on a tour of some of the western US national parks when Dad saw an impromptu video that Samaritan's Purse had posted online of me asking for helpers, prayer, and financial support. He said my plea for assistance got to him, and Dad arranged to come sooner to work with us.

∾

I took Amber and the kids to the airport on July 20. She texted me the next morning from the airport in London. "A bit stressful here," I told her, "but everything is okay."

We exchanged our next texts on Tuesday, July 22. The family was in Abilene and adjusting to the jet lag. "I am tired, but I love you," I texted. Then I shared exciting news with Amber: Dr. Ian Jackson had informed me that he could come work with us in Liberia for four weeks, beginning as early as the following Sunday.

Ian and I had been colleagues in residency and remained good friends. He was a year behind me in training and had graduated from his fellowship at JPS in June. We had been desperately seeking someone to replace me in the hospital, because I had become consumed with my duties in the ETU, and that left a physician gap in the hospital.

We had fewer than ten doctors to begin with, and part of my job at the hospital had been to take obstetrics call, do ultrasounds, and make rounds. John Fankhauser was the only other doctor who did ultrasounds and took OB call, but he was already carrying too heavy a load: filling in for the hospital administrator and working shifts in the ETU.

A number of SP volunteers had arrived to help, but none of them possessed my particular skill set, so we needed someone to handle my duties in the regular hospital in order to take some of the load off John. I recognized that what we needed was a JPS-trained doctor. I reached out to David McRay and other colleagues, then I also contacted Ian. Thank the Lord, Ian had agreed to join us.

∾

On Sunday, July 20, the same day that Amber and the kids left for the States, Scott Parker, one of my best friends in Fort Worth, sent me an encouraging text telling me that Randy Harris had spoken at our church in Fort Worth, Southside Church of Christ.

Randy was a theology and philosophy professor at Abilene Christian. As an undergraduate student I had taken a couple of his classes and participated in a mentoring group he sponsored. Later, Randy also had connected with my brother Kerry.

Scott's text said he had thought of me during that morning's message. Randy had shared from Romans 8:28: "And we know that in all things God works for the good of those who love him, who have been called according to his purpose."

"He said among other things," Scott's text read, "that the promise of God working in all things is that whatever we are going through, it is not final and you are not alone. I thought of you. Perhaps with whatever you are seeing and doing each day, it is encouraging to know that it is not final and you are not alone. Love you guys. Praying for you."

8

Just Not Feeling Right

Kent

Wednesday, July 23, I woke up just after 6 a.m., and I did not feel right. I didn't have any specific illness, but I felt hot, and when I went to the bathroom, I had a rather loose stool. I took my temperature, and it was 100.0. Our cutoff in screening patients for Ebola had been 100.4, so my temperature was not to the point of being febrile, but it was above normal.

I wasn't concerned, though, because I had worked long hours the previous three days, even compared with the hectic schedule I had maintained for seven weeks. Plus, the night before, Eric Buller, a SIM missionary whose family lived next door to us, had needed to finish making homemade pepperoni pizzas in our oven because theirs had run out of propane. Eric and I had shared one of the pizzas. I put a heavy dose of Tabasco sauce on my pizza, even though that often causes me to have an upset stomach the next day. To me, eating pizza with Tabasco sauce was one of those risk-reward decisions where the reward outweighed the risk.

I showered, brushed my teeth, and dressed for work. I rechecked my temperature. It was 99.8.

"Hey, I don't feel good this morning," I told Lance Plyler by phone. "I don't know what it is—maybe I have a cold or it might be something I ate last night. But

I think the best thing is for me to just stay home until it blows over, and I think I will be better later today. But I will do some administrative work this morning and come in later."

"Okay, that's cool," Lance said. "Do you have any diarrhea or have you been vomiting? Do you have any other symptoms?"

"No," I answered. "I'm fine."

"Call me at lunchtime and tell me how you are doing. Do you need me to bring you a rapid malaria test?" Lance asked.

"No, I have a box of them in my closet. I will do one later."

If I had been working in a hospital back in Fort Worth or in Indianapolis, I absolutely would have gone to work despite how I felt. No hesitation. But in the middle of what was becoming the world's worst Ebola outbreak, I chose to stay home, at least for the morning, to ride out whatever I had. There was no reason for me to think I had Ebola, but I knew where I was and I knew the danger of having Ebola yet carrying on with business as usual, then exposing a bunch of other people in the process. I had watched that scenario play out repeatedly for the past seven weeks.

I was not so naive to think I could not contract Ebola. But I did not stay home because I thought I had Ebola. I stayed home because I did not feel good and knew that was the safest, and right, thing to do.

I sat down on my bed and worked on my laptop. I actually accomplished a great deal. I am easily distracted when on a computer, especially by Facebook and YouTube, but I was particularly focused and productive that morning.

As newly appointed medical director of the consolidated treatment unit, I was responsible for staffing, scheduling, and training. I had spent numerous hours over the past week with Cokie van der Velde, a British hygiene expert with MSF, and kou Leanue Bamakpa, a Liberian with SP Liberia who was the designated human resources person for the project. Both were helping me prepare for the opening of ELWA 2.

That morning I worked on the schedule for the expatriates coming to us through SP, completed e-mail correspondence, and wished a friend back in the States a happy birthday through Facebook.

I also gave myself a rapid diagnostic test (RDT) for malaria. All missionaries kept a box of RDTs in their homes. It's a simple test—just a quick finger prick to get a drop of blood on a test strip. Fifteen minutes later, you can read the result. My test came back negative.

A little later I took another malaria test. That one also was negative.

The negative tests did not concern me. We saw three strains of malaria in West Africa, and the test was for the worst of those—plasmodium falciparum. The tests are 99 percent specific and 99 percent sensitive, thus incredibly accurate. But if I had one of the other two strains, the test would show negative.

At lunchtime I felt a little feverish and checked my temperature again. It was 101.4.

Still I was not concerned. Being medically febrile did not tip me off to anything except that I was sick with something. I still thought I had malaria, because it is so prevalent in West Africa. Everyone in our family took an antimalarial Malarone pill every day, and I was certain I had missed a few doses due to my crazy schedule. Also, I had seen malaria present itself in many different ways in patients and in other missionaries, including Amber, who had caught it in June.

I called Lance and told him I had a fever. He said he would send someone to my house a little later to draw blood for an Ebola test.

TESTED FOR EBOLA

It took a few hours for someone to arrive. I was not surprised. For one, whoever would come would have to leave the isolation unit. They were very busy there, and arrangements would have to be made to cover for anyone who was gone.

Second, I learned later, there were discussions on how they could come to my house and suit up in Tychem (PPE) suits without anyone seeing them. I was the medical director of the unit. I had been there from the beginning and had been telling everyone that our procedures were safe—that if we followed protocols, did everything the way we had been trained, and worked together as a team, we all would be safe.

I had told them there was no reason to be afraid of working in the isolation unit. In fact I said that working in the ER was scarier and more dangerous, because in the isolation unit we were all suited up and *knew* we were working with patients who either had Ebola or were suspected of having it. In the ER we had no idea what diseases would come through the doors. For that matter, I was confident that working in the Ebola unit was safer at that point than going to market or to church.

So there was special concern over how the Liberians on the staff would react to hearing that I was sick and people wearing PPE had walked into my home.

I was sitting on the living-room couch when Dr. Nathalie MacDermott, Dr. Alicia Chilito, and Bev Kauffeldt arrived on the porch. Nathalie and Alicia had recently come to Liberia through SP Disaster Response. Bev, the wife of Kendell, SP's country director in Liberia, had returned to Monrovia the previous weekend after spending four weeks in Foya as the head hygienist for the Ebola treatment unit there.

I had unlocked the front door and moved a basket of shoes and a small coffee table away from the door so they would have more room and would not have to touch anything when they entered. From the couch, I told them I had touched the back of the door but nothing else in that area.

They opened the door but did not enter. Not wearing suits to prevent raising suspicions, Bev sprayed our tile floor with the bleach mix before stepping inside to spray the back of the door. Nathalie and Alicia followed her in and then started to suit up. I watched as they put on the yellow Tychem suits, which are a little heavier duty PPE than the white ones we also wore. I hated those yellow suits because they were made of plastic and were bulky.

I knew the fifteen-minute routine well: boots, suit, two pairs of gloves, apron, mask, extra hood for the head, and last but not least goggles. When they had completed the process, Nathalie came over to the couch to draw my blood.

The mood in the living room was surreal, and I tried to lighten the atmosphere.

"You know," I joked, "if you are worried about doing this, I could draw my own blood."

Nathalie asked from which arm I wanted her to take blood. I am right-handed and prefer to get stuck in the opposite arm. Because we had run out of formal tourniquets at the hospital, she used a rubber glove to make a tourniquet on my left arm, stuck me with a needle, drew my blood, and set the vial on the armrest of the couch.

"Oh, now you've contaminated the couch," Bev said. "I am going to have to spray that."

"Bev," I said, "please don't spray my couch. If I have Ebola, the whole thing is contaminated and we'll have to burn it. But if I don't have Ebola, it is not contaminated, and there is no reason to ruin it with bleach. Can we wait?"

Bev spared the couch.

I don't think any of us believed I had Ebola. I still speculated malaria. But the four of us knew we had to take every precaution, as though I did have Ebola, until we proved otherwise.

Nathalie prepared to label the vial.

"How are we going to do this?" I asked her. "You can't send a vial of blood to be tested for Ebola with my name on it. Darlington Komosee, one of the main guys in the lab, works at our hospital. I have been working with him for nine months. He is one of my best friends here."

"We will give you a Liberian name," Bev suggested. "What is your birth-order number?" She had lived in Liberia for ten years. The tribe she was most familiar with based children's names on birth order, and she had learned those names.

"I am number six."

"Never mind," Bev said. She had not learned that far down the list of names. "How about Tamba? That is a common name. What is your mother's maiden name? We will make that your last name."

"Snell," I replied.

Nathalie wrote *Tamba Snell* on the vial.

I could not fathom the mental and emotional burden the three of them labored under, coming into my house for the purpose of giving me an Ebola test.

Amber and I had known Bev and her husband, Kendell, since we had moved to Liberia. Bev was not a medical person. She had a PhD and specialized in water and sanitation, particularly how to provide clean water and latrines for communities. But she had spent an intense month in Foya, the Liberian epicenter of the initial Ebola outbreak, where conditions had been far worse than in Monrovia. As a hygienist, in addition to spraying the bleach decontaminant, she had placed dead bodies in body bags and carried them out of the isolation unit. What she had witnessed in Foya had been horrifically graphic.

I had not worked with Nathalie and Alicia long, but I had given them their orientation after their arrival in Liberia.

While we waited on the results of yet another malaria test, I watched them go through the very detailed process of removing their suits—*doffing their gear* is the technical term, but we always called it decontaminating. I had trained them in the process, and I knew they suddenly had to be wondering if what we had been doing all along was indeed completely safe.

"NEVER DOUBT MALARIA"

The rapid malaria test—my third one—was negative. The blood sample would need to be sent to the lab for an Ebola test.

I was already starting to grow irritated, because I knew I would have to be isolated for three days. I thought this whole ordeal was a waste of time with so much work that needed to be done at the hospital, and my being out for three days would cause my colleagues' workloads to increase.

Tamba Snell's vial of blood was placed inside a bag and inside another bag, then into a cooler of sorts. Nathalie, Alicia, and Bev finished decontaminating and placed their suits in a trash bag, which they left in the house. Bev sprayed every spot where they had been in my living room. Then she sprayed across my feet and the three of them left.

I began making phone calls.

I asked Lance Plyler when the test results would be available. He could not give me an answer because he did not know when the lab guys would come and pick up the test and take it back to National Reference Labs. The lab was forty minutes away and the only place in Liberia that handled Ebola tests. It was not safe to run tests on potential Ebola blood in a regular lab.

I called my next-door neighbor, Eric Buller. "Eric, I need to tell you something, and I need you to not tell your wife because my wife does not know. I have a fever. I am sick. I don't feel very well. They just came and drew blood for an Ebola test. I wanted you to know because people are going to be coming and going, and I want you to know what is going on. And I want you to pray for me."

Dr. Debbie and I had been partners and coworkers during the outbreak, and as SIM's medical liaison, she was the person to whom the missionaries reported anytime we were sick. It was her job to treat anyone on the team who was ill. I called Debbie to tell her that I was not feeling well and had isolated myself at home.

The first person I called back in the United States was Scott Parker in Fort Worth. He and his wife, Tricia, headed up our home support network. Scott did not answer, so I sent him a text to let him know it had been me who had called and that I would call him again shortly. I asked him to please answer when I called. He responded twenty or thirty minutes later, apologizing for having his phone on silent and missing my call. He was at work but said I could call him and he would step out to take the call.

Our conversation was short. I told Scott that I had a fever but did not think I had Ebola. I told him I was not going to call Amber until the next day when "I had a negative test result," so she would not worry. I asked for him and a couple of our friends, Johny and Philip, to pray for me.

At some point during those calls—I think the one with Lance, but I am not sure—I learned that Nancy Writebol had malaria. The day before, Tuesday, had been her birthday, and she had asked on Monday if I needed her to work the next day. We had transitioned to the new unit, and that had changed up the teams and our processes.

"I'm happy to work," she'd said, "but I don't want to be in the way."

"What do you want to do?" I asked.

"I want to be here," she answered. "I want to help, but I don't want to work all day Tuesday."

Her husband, David, hoped to take her out for a birthday dinner, so she did not want to put in a typical twelve-hour day. We decided she would work a short day and take off in time for dinner.

Because I was so busy on Tuesday, I did not know that Nancy had not felt well at work and had gone home that afternoon. Dr. Debbie had given her a malaria test that came back positive.

Learning this about Nancy gave me more hope that I had malaria too. Nancy and I both had been working long hours and a lot of night shifts, and I could have easily forgotten to take my daily dose of Malarone. Also, there were a ton of mosquitoes outside ELWA 1, because we had barrels and buckets stacked outside that collected water during the rainy season. I had dumped some water out of barrels and buckets one day, and I could see mosquito larvae in the stagnant water. It was very possible that I had been bitten by mosquitoes and gotten malaria like Nancy.

Still sitting in bed, and after completing the calls I needed to make, I debated whether I should work more or take a nap. I was texting with Eric at the time and asked what he thought I should do.

"You should work," he said. "But if it were me, I would watch a movie."

I had not developed any specific symptoms, but I felt hot and was growing tired. Instead of working or sleeping, I decided to watch a movie: *Black Hawk Down*. It was a poor choice to watch a modern war movie loaded with death, but we had borrowed a handful of DVDs from Dr. Debbie, and I knew that Amber would not watch that movie with me. *Black Hawk Down* was not a light or uplifting movie!

After the movie I took a nap.

Around 5 p.m., Dr. Debbie came over to my house with a batch of homemade lemon bars she had baked that afternoon. She stood on the front porch and carefully handed the plate to me, with me grabbing the opposite end from what she was holding. Debbie had placed a small note on the lemon bars to lift my spirits. The card read "EVD RTUF." "Ebola Virus Disease Ready to Use Food," she said, like it was military rations. We both had a good laugh.

Joni Byker, the senior program manager for SP Liberia, brought me a dinner of chicken and dressing. Like Debbie, she did not come inside, and we made a distant hand-off of the dishes.

Joni looked at me with an "I don't know what to say" face. It was weird to see that look from someone I had worked closely with. She told me that she would be praying for me, and I thanked her for dinner.

Her chicken and dressing was so tasty that I ate every bite of it. I sent her a text: "Thanks for dinner. It was delicious. I ate all of it. I will return your dishes in three days." I just knew that my Ebola test would come back negative and I would be cleared to return to work, so I could give Joni's dishes back to her in person. I couldn't have Ebola, because I knew of no possible exposure.

I called John Fankhauser, and his wife, Beth, answered his cell phone. John was swimming in the ocean trying to catch a few minutes of peace away from the stress at the hospital, and he had left his phone at home. I did not tell Beth anything was wrong, just that I wanted to talk to John. She informed me that they were hosting the Wednesday night SIM missionary prayer gathering later that evening. Amber and I had hosted the previous week's meeting at our house, where I was now isolated.

I also talked by phone with Lance about whether I should start taking malaria medicine. All the missionaries kept oral medication for malaria in their homes— right next to the RDTs.

"I don't think you have malaria, because you've had three negative tests," he told me.

"Lance," I said, "you may doubt malaria, but I have been living here for nine months, and I have learned to never doubt malaria. I don't care what the tests say. When someone is sick with a febrile illness, it is malaria until proven otherwise. And what is the risk of me taking the medicine? It has a very low side-effect profile."

We ended the call without making a decision, and he later texted me to say, "I agree. You should go ahead and start taking it."

"Well," I texted back, "I already did."

I had called Amber and the kids every day since they had arrived in Texas, and I debated whether I should call them that day. I did not want to tell her that I had not been feeling well until I also could tell her that my Ebola test was negative.

My decision was made for me around 9 p.m., when after writing in my journal, I fell asleep.

Amber

I drove the kids to San Angelo, Texas, on Wednesday morning, about a ninety-mile trip southwest from Abilene. Kent's brother, Chad, is a dentist there, and he gave us checkups and his hygienist cleaned our teeth. The kids and I went to lunch with Chad and saw his baby girl, Sydney, for the first time.

We ate at Cork and Pig Tavern, a restaurant we visited every trip to San Angelo. During the meal, I looked at the time on my phone. Liberia is five hours ahead of Texas, so it was evening in Monrovia.

"Kent has not called me all day today, that little stinker," I said.

Chad laughed, then we resumed our conversation.

The kids and I drove back to Abilene that night, and I still had not heard from Kent. I wondered why he had not called, considering we had talked every day, but I knew how busy he was and didn't think much of it.

Kent

Despite my feeling worse as the day progressed, Wednesday turned out to be a really good day. I spent time reading Scripture and from Oswald Chambers's *My*

Utmost for His Highest devotional, which Ed Carns had given me when he stayed with me in April. I wrote in my journal,

> I guess I have a few days to rest now. But this is not the complete rest. As the Hebrew writer said, "Today, if you hear his voice, do not harden your hearts as you did in the rebellion."[5] The promise of entering his rest still stands, so let us never give up. Let us, therefore, make every effort— *spoudazo*—make every effort to enter that rest.[6]

I had written *spoudazo* in the margin of my Bible once during a class. It is the Greek word for "to make every effort."

Then I wrote a Scripture from Hebrews: "Let us then approach the throne of grace *with confidence,* so that we may receive mercy and find grace to help us in our time of need."[7]

I wrote *with confidence* in italics.

Inspired by a song I had long loved, I concluded, "In my life, Lord, be glorified today."

I did not feel that way every day that I lived in Liberia, but that was the type of reflection I carried into my illness. I count it as a gift from God that I experienced that devotional time on Wednesday, because I had no idea that I was taking my first step onto my personal battlefield with Ebola.

9

Praying for Dengue Fever

Kent

The test for Tamba Snell had come back: negative for Ebola. I was not surprised when I received the results on Thursday. That was what I expected. But I also knew the result meant practically nothing.

It can take up to seventy-two hours for Ebola to show up in a test. Protocol in our treatment unit had been that a negative test in the first three days of illness was considered indeterminate. We always disregarded that negative and continued treating the patient as though she had Ebola. We tested only to see if we received a positive. If a positive result came back within the first three days, we knew for sure what we were dealing with. Otherwise, we waited until finding out the results of a second test.

The true test would come Saturday when I would be retested. My mind-set until then was that as long as I had a negative, I did not have a positive.

So maybe I really have malaria even though the tests were all negative. Or maybe I have dengue fever?

Dengue fever is a miserable sickness. We saw it in West Africa, but it was not common. Dengue fever is a weird, tropical disease that, like malaria, is transmitted through mosquitoes. It is similar to malaria, but also can cause a hemorrhagic fever and severe body aches. It is sometimes called break-bone fever, because when patients are stricken with it, they feel like their bones are breaking. There is no treatment for dengue fever, but most people survive it, especially the first time they have it. No one would hope to have dengue fever. However, faced with the possibility that I could have Ebola, I prayed that I had dengue fever.

John Fankhauser had texted me that morning to ask how I was doing. I felt lousy, more tired than the day before. In light of the negative Ebola test, we discussed the possibility that I could have dengue. We decided to continue my treatment for malaria despite the negative tests. We also started antibiotics to cover any other infection I might have.

John told me that Beth had made chicken-noodle soup and that he would bring me some shortly. When he came, he handed me the soup through the front door. I was standing there talking to him when an overwhelming wave of nausea hit me unlike anything I had ever experienced before.

"I think I have to sit down," I told John.

I backed up, set the soup on the coffee table, and plopped down on the couch. The next thing I knew, I was rolling back and forth on the couch, moaning, with my skin feeling clammy and turning pale. John stood in the doorway and watched; because he was not wearing PPE, he could not come in to help me.

The nausea lasted only a few minutes, and once I had regained my composure, John left. Much later I learned that after John had seen how poorly I looked on my couch, he told someone at the hospital, "I think Kent has Ebola. There is something not normal going on here."

After the nausea resolved, I ate Beth's soup and spent most of the day dozing off and on. I checked my temperature early in the afternoon, and my fever had jumped to 103.2. I took Tylenol, and at the next check, I was back down to 100.4.

I called Amber around midday.

Amber

Kent's voice sounded normal, but he told me he had been sick and running a fever, plus he had a headache, body aches, eye pain, and fatigue. He didn't pause before telling me about the negative Ebola test, the negative malaria tests, and how he and

John had decided to treat him with antibiotics and medication for malaria, while hoping that maybe he had dengue fever.

Hearing how sick he felt knocked the wind out of me. I've heard how the wife of a soldier feels when her husband has been wounded in battle and is laid up in a field hospital—thousands of miles from her loving arms. I felt like that. I hated that I was not there to take care of him. I wanted to see him and know that he was all right.

My parents are house parents at a children's home in Abilene, and they were on a youth retreat with their seven teenage foster kids when Kent called. They returned later that afternoon, and I waited until the teenagers weren't around, while we were sitting at the table, to tell them, "Kent is sick. They tested him for Ebola, which was negative. They have to wait three more days to test him again, and he has to be in isolation until his second test. But you should just know that he is sick and pray for him."

We did not tell any other members of our family, including Ruby and Stephen. I knew Kent would be isolated until Saturday, when he would be tested again for Ebola. I also knew how crucial that test was. Aware that we would be in limbo the next two days over Kent's health, I did not want to cause panic among the family. I wanted everyone to keep preparing for my brother's wedding. I wanted everything to be as normal as possible for everyone else, even though it wouldn't be for me. I worried about Kent. I worried about that next Ebola test.

Ebola was like the proverbial elephant in the room for me. I tried to push it back in my mind, I tried to have faith that Kent had something else, but I knew Ebola was a real possibility.

Before falling asleep, I wrote in my journal about my conversation with Kent. My final words were,

I fear more his dying than death myself. I fear being a single mother. I fear losing Kent six years into our marriage. I fear for my kids growing up without their Daddy.

Lord, help us.

I slept horribly that night. I dreamed I was sitting in a memorial service for Kent at our church in Fort Worth. All the seats on the floor and in the balcony were filled to overflowing, with people standing in the aisles and in the back of the sanctuary. I couldn't stop crying. I have a close friend named Charla Hilligoss whose husband had passed away a year earlier. Charla was in my dream, holding me for a long time during the service. But still the tears flowed.

A little before 5 a.m. Friday, I texted Kent, "I'm awake." It was almost 10 a.m. in Monrovia and I thought he would be up too.

"Do you want to FaceTime?" he texted back.

We did, and Kent looked really tired. He said he still felt bad and had a fever of 102. He also was bored and lonely.

I told him about my dream.

"I don't feel like I'm dying," he said.

THE EVIDENCE MOUNTS

Kent

Amber did not say she was scared when we talked, but I am her husband—I could tell she was scared. I wanted to sound strong for her, and I believed that if I did have Ebola, I would feel worse than I did. That is why I told her I did not feel like I was dying.

I was, however, feeling worse than the day before. Along with that, I had less hope that I had malaria than the day before, because I had been on antimalarial medication for two days and would expect symptoms from malaria to be improving, not getting worse.

My temperature reached 104 on Friday morning. John and Nathalie came to see me before noon because John wanted to start me on IV antibiotics. Nathalie started the IV line, and they gave me two grams of ceftriaxone, a broad-spectrum antibiotic used to treat a number of bacterial infections, and then began IV fluids.

I did not feel dehydrated, but John wanted to get out ahead of any fluid loss I might experience, because we had observed Ebola patients who produced so much diarrhea that we were unable to keep them sufficiently hydrated. As I look back, that move by John might have been one of the most critical decisions made early in my care.

We had given some patients twelve liters of fluid a day, which was a lot. Without the automatic pumps, we had to stand next to the bed and squeeze the IV bag until we could infuse all the fluid. That could take anywhere from fifteen to forty-five minutes. We could not hang an IV bag and walk away, because if a patient went to the bathroom, got out of bed to throw up, or became delirious and started rolling around, he could pull the IV out and bleed. Bleeding was dangerous for the patient, not to mention the doctors and nurses.

Doctors tend to make lousy patients, and I certainly am no exception. But at least I knew how to work the IV, so John did not have to stand there and squeeze all the fluids into me. He did give me some fluid as a bolus, though—squeezing it into me so I would receive a large dose in a short amount of time to quicken its effect.

Nathalie left shortly after the IV had started, while John remained with me for an hour or so. My head pounded, and I felt weak and a little out of it. I had asked for homemade yogurt on Thursday, and the Bullers made a batch for me. John brought the yogurt with him, and I ate some. The last time I checked my temperature when John was with me, it registered at 103.4.

I called my parents and told them that I was sick with a fever but had tested negative for Ebola. I received text messages from family members and close friends. I did not know how much word was spreading back home that I was sick, but I wasn't bombarded with texts because Amber and I communicated back to the United States through Viber, a free phone-call and text-messaging app. Only those who had Viber were able to send me a message. Normally, I love having company. The more people in the room, the merrier. But as I began to feel worse, I did not have the energy—physical or mental—to engage in long conversations.

Early Friday afternoon, I had diarrhea for the first time. I had been on Lonart, an oral medication for malaria, for two-and-a-half days. Because I still was running a high fever, John wanted to give me maximal treatment for malaria using IV artesunate. That was the only IV malaria medicine we gave Ebola patients, because the other IV malaria medicines had too many side effects that matched the symptoms of Ebola, clouding the clinical picture and making it impossible to determine whether the patient was dealing with side effects of the medicine or the Ebola was worsening.

We had run out of IV artesunate at ELWA, though, and John called William Sulonteh, the hospital pharmacist, and asked him to do whatever he could to find a course of treatment. Outside of a select few, no one knew I was sick. I was still Tamba Snell, so John could not tell William that the course was for me.

"Treat it as though you are trying to find the medicine for your mother or your brother," John told him.

Mr. Sulonteh did just that, spending much of his day looking for a course of artesunate. He struck out at five pharmacies he contacted, along with JFK and Redemption Hospital in New Kru Town. Finally, around 3 p.m., he located a course at the national tuberculosis hospital in Monrovia and was able to convince them to give it to him. William returned with the medicine during the afternoon.

An hour later, John suited up at my house and started me on the IV artesunate.

THANKFUL FOR GATORADE AND TANG

Gatorade is a luxury in Monrovia. I asked for some anyway. In the treatment unit we wanted patients to take as much oral hydration as possible to accompany the IV fluids, so we gave them what is called ORS, oral rehydration solution. It was an electrolyte powder we mixed with water, usually orange flavored. I would call it a homemade Gatorade, but that would imply that it tasted like Gatorade. And I do not want to be accused of claiming that.

ORS tasted awful. Horrendously awful. Earlier in July I had been inside the Ebola treatment unit wearing PPE for about four hours. It was the longest I had stayed inside a suit, and I was drenched with sweat. My scrubs underneath felt like I had jumped into a swimming pool. Nancy was outside the unit serving as our decontamination person and runner, and I told her I would want some ORS when I came out so I would not get too dehydrated.

I exited the unit, went through the decontamination process, and took a drink of ORS. It tasted like warm ocean water. I did not take another sip and drank water instead. I could not believe that our patients actually were able to drink that stuff.

When I became ill, I was advised to drink ORS.

"No way!" I said. "I am not drinking that. Bring me Gatorade."

I honestly did not believe that I would be able to stomach enough of the ORS to stay hydrated. Dr. Debbie brought me Tang powder, and others made sure I had a supply of Gatorade.

Those who were coming into my house to take care of me would pour me a cup of Tang or give me a bottle of Gatorade. I was feeling so poorly that I requested that my supplies be set up in a specific order on the nightstand next to my bed. I had exact spots for my thermometer, my bottle of water, my Gatorade and Tang, my next dose of medicine, and a bottle of Tylenol.

"You're awful particular," my friends would tease me.

I wasn't being particular; I was being practical. I was so weakened that I needed all those things within reach so that I would not have to expend the energy required to get out of bed to find them.

Although there was more traffic into and out of my house than usual, we tried to be as discreet as possible to prevent any speculation and rumors. Our house had a back door that I could have opened and carried on conversations through, but I did not feel strong enough to get up and go to the back door. Instead, I cracked open the bedroom window beyond the foot of my bed and opened the curtain about a foot so that anyone who came by could communicate with me through the window. I'm afraid I was not good company, because I could not stay awake long before falling back asleep.

John had to perform a C-section at the hospital that night, and afterward he returned to my house to give me more fluids. He stayed until probably 2 a.m. to make sure I received all the medications I needed when they were due.

Amber sent me a text that night. We often talked to each other in Spanish, and she told me, "Goodnight, *mi amor.* Take care."

Amber

Friday was a long day. I just could not get out of my mind how sick Kent was. He sincerely believed he did not have Ebola. But at ELWA I had visited the hospital to take water and food to Kent and others working in the isolation unit, and he had been sharing with me the descriptions of Ebola patients. Kent and I have talked medicine together our entire marriage. Because I am a nurse, Kent could come home from work and talk about cases with me, and I would understand what he was describing. Those two months we had been living under the Ebola outbreak, he *had* to talk to someone. It was too stressful not to.

As a result, I wasn't ignorant when it came to Ebola.

I couldn't know if Kent had Ebola, but I could pray he had malaria or dengue fever, as odd as that sounds. We would not learn anything new until Kent's test on Saturday, but I knew my husband was very, very sick.

That night I journaled,

He can't die. I can't raise these kids on my own. They need their daddy.
I need their daddy.

PART 4

TESTED POSITIVE

10

Kent . . . Has . . . Ebola

Kent

I had to text Amber. It was 7 a.m. Saturday morning, so 2 a.m. in Texas, and I knew that Amber kept her phone on silent overnight and a text message would not wake her. I wanted her to wake up to good news.

"My temp is 100.2 this morning. Thank God!"

Three and a half hours later, I sent another text: "Are you awake?"

Just after 6 a.m., she texted to say she had just woken up and that we could talk a little later.

By the time John came to check on me that morning and Nathalie had come to draw blood for my second Ebola test, my temperature had dropped to 99 degrees and my nausea had lessened. John sprayed out at noon and informed Dr. Debbie that my condition had improved.

At about 3 p.m., my temperature had jumped back up to 103.4. I notified John.

"On my way," he replied.

Amber

I was a nervous wreck Saturday. I didn't know when to expect to hear the results of Kent's second Ebola test, but it sat heavy on my mind all day.

We have a family tradition of gathering for coffee at my grandparents' house on Saturday mornings. Happy and Papa had dug deep into a closet to find the toys I had played with at their house as a child. Ruby and Stephen had a great time, and seeing them with those toys brought back pleasant memories for me.

It was a pretty large gathering of people at Happy and Papa's, because people were coming to see me and the kids while we were in town, plus there were discussions to have and plans to make regarding the wedding the following Saturday.

Only my parents knew Kent was sick, and that's the way I wanted it until we knew whether or not he had Ebola.

As we all drank coffee around the kitchen table, I was distracted and tuning in and out of the conversation. My dad kept looking over at me or patting me on the shoulder when he was standing near me because he knew how worried I was. He was worried about Kent too.

I think I actually spent more time away from the table than with everyone, because I just wasn't much for talking. I sat in the floor with the kids and played Candy Land, trying to appear cool and collected. But the whole time, that test loomed over me.

Kent

John spent the afternoon with me. That night, a little after 8 p.m., he woke me up from a nap.

I awoke in a state of confusion, like when something startles you in the middle of a deep slumber and you are so disoriented that you do not know what time it is or what is going on. I thought John was waking me up to tell me he was leaving my house. Actually, he had left while I was asleep and had just returned with Lance Plyler. I had been so sound asleep that I was not aware John had been gone.

After I looked up at John to my right, I noticed Lance outside my bedroom window. I sat up in bed, propping myself against the headboard. I was still trying to clear my mind when Lance, in a matter-of-fact but gentle voice, broke the news: "Kent, bud. We got your test results. And I'm really sorry to tell you that it is positive for Ebola."

I don't recall how Lance and John answered when I asked about our plan. I remember John stepping out of my bedroom to leave me alone when I called Amber, but not even the phone call itself is in my memory.

Amber

My phone rang at 4 p.m. in Abilene. We had returned to my parents' house, and I hurried to the bedroom where I could have privacy.

"The test results came back," Kent said. "It's positive."

I didn't know how to respond, and I sensed Kent was waiting for me to say something.

"I'm so sorry," I told him. That was all I could say.

I started to cry. Kent didn't cry. He told me several times how much peace he felt. He was so calm. We didn't stay on the phone long, just a few minutes. He hadn't been able to talk long before because of his weakness and fatigue, and he said he had more calls to make. We said we loved each other and hung up.

I laid across the bed and cried for several minutes. I went into the bathroom, dried my face with a hand towel, and returned to sit on the bed.

I sent my dad a text: "Daddy."

That was all I knew to say. That was all I needed to say.

Dad came quickly into the bedroom, followed by Mom. I didn't tell them anything. They knew. They sat beside me on the bed and we wept. It felt like we were on the bed for a long time, holding each other and crying.

We were interrupted by a phone call from Franklin Graham, the president and CEO of Samaritan's Purse. Neither Kent nor I had ever met or talked with Franklin.

"Amber, this is Franklin Graham."

He was slow to speak.

"I don't know what to say, because I can't tell you everything is going to be all right. But we are going to do everything we can to take care of Kent. My wife and I are praying for you."

I thanked him for his prayers and concern.

"I don't know if you realize this," he continued. "This is a big international news story."

"No," I replied. "I hadn't thought of that."

Franklin told me that the communications team at Samaritan's Purse would be in touch soon to help me.

I had no idea how big the story would become—that it would capture the attention of the world. Or how soon that would happen.

Kent

Immediately after talking with Amber, I called my parents. Because of the high fever, to this day I have almost a sort of amnesia. There are details from that period that I cannot remember, and I recall little about that phone call with my parents.

My oldest sister, Carole, and her whole family were visiting my parents, and my nephew Brantly Houston was living there that summer while he served an internship in Indianapolis.

I asked my parents if everyone was in the house and told them they should gather together in a private place. Carole's husband, Duwain, took their youngest son outside while we talked. All I remember from the conversation is that everyone on their end of the call was crying. As when I had told Amber, I did not cry. Even now when I think about telling my parents I had tested positive, I tear up. But that day, I did not.

My mom called the rest of my brothers and sisters and relayed the news to them. I spoke with all of them at some point that night. I also remember that I called Scott Parker and David McRay back in Fort Worth to tell them and ask them to pray.

I did not know at the time that our neighbors in the duplex, Jake and Melanie Neiss and their two young children, had been forced to move out after my diagnosis. Our front doors were right next to each other, and Melanie had been kind enough to make a pitcher of Tang for me when I requested one and slipped it inside my front door. Kendell Kauffeldt called Jake and Melanie after my test came back positive to tell them they had five minutes to get out of their side of the duplex.

I felt terrible when I learned about it, because they essentially lost all their belongings because of me, even though I had not been in their house and nothing they had could have become contaminated with Ebola. With the benefit of hindsight, it seems unnecessary that they had to move. But everything about our situation was unprecedented, and we could not take too many precautions.

HYMNS AND PRAYERS

Amber

That evening we had a small birthday party for my brother Kevin. I remember my grandparents being there along with a couple of siblings. Fortunately, that day wasn't Kevin's actual birthday. That would have been some birthday to celebrate.

The children's home where my parents live is situated on a beautiful campus, and I decided to take a walk in search of a quiet spot where I could spend some time alone and process what was happening. I walked across a field and through a group of mesquite trees. I stopped at a pipe-rail fence, and a couple of horses the home uses for equine therapy walked toward me. One came right up to me and let me hold it and pet it for as long as I wanted. Standing beside that fence, with a hand on the horse's head, I had a time of quiet and peace that I needed. That horse did me a big favor.

Mesquite trees, especially in that part of West Texas, can grow out wiry and gnarled. One tree had a big, low branch that stretched out parallel to the ground at a height a little above that of a porch swing. I climbed up to sit on that branch. Being late July in Texas, it was quite warm out. But in the shade of that tree, it was pleasant.

I had taken my phone with me because Kent and I would text each other from time to time to check on each other. News about Kent was beginning to get out, and friends were sending me texts and e-mails. I looked through some of those messages. Most were recommending Bible verses for me to read. When I came across those who had pasted the text of the verse in their message, I read the Scripture.

I remember reading these words of Paul: "I want to know Christ and the power of his resurrection and the fellowship of sharing in his sufferings, becoming like him in his death, and so, somehow, to attain to the resurrection from the dead."[8]

Kent and I were both suffering, in very different ways. I felt a bond with Kent over our suffering and found comfort in these other words Paul wrote: "For to me, to live is Christ and to die is gain."[9]

Hymns started coming to mind, like "Be with Me, Lord." I looked up the lyrics on my phone. The song begins, "Be with me, Lord. I cannot live without Thee."[10] I looked up "Great Is Thy Faithfulness" and pasted the lyrics into the notes app on my phone. What a powerful message in that moment to sing to myself,

Thou changest not, Thy compassions, they fail not.
As Thou hast been Thou forever wilt be.[11]

I couldn't formulate prayers on my own. Those hymns became my prayers.

Then I thought of another hymn that had held special meaning to Kent and, later, to us as a family.

In 2006 Kent had made a mission trip to Honduras. He had a phone that the missionaries had given him to carry for intergroup communication. While in a small clinic in a mountain village, he received a phone call from back home. His grandfather had unexpectedly died of a heart attack.

Kent made plans to return home for the funeral, and the next day he boarded a flight back to the United States. He had a CD player with him and one CD by

Photo by Tammy Marcelain

Our wedding day, May 29, 2008.

Photo by Bethany Fankhauser

Our family on ELWA beach, December 2013, Monrovia, Liberia.

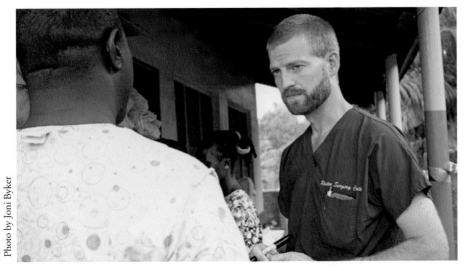

Kent working with hospital staff outside of ELWA 1.

Kent (left) caring for a patient in ELWA 1. Personal protective equipment and no stethoscope or watch make measuring vital signs very challenging.

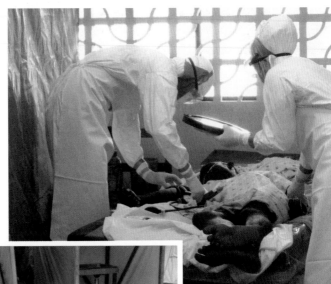

Kent washing dishes at ELWA 1.

Kent, Gebah, Dr. Debbie Eisenhut, and Nancy Writebol.

Dr. Lance Plyler standing outside Kent's bedroom window, checking on him.

Dr. Lance Plyler holding the foam cooler that contained ZMapp.

Kent sitting up after the administration of ZMapp.

Photo by Brett Fitch

People all over the world prayed for Kent. Our home church in Fort Worth joined hands in prayer after Kent's diagnosis.

Photo by Brett Fitch

Photo by Dr. Lance Plyler

The care team from Samaritan's Purse outside the Brantlys' home, praying for Kent after he left on the evacuation airplane.

Together again at last in the isolation unit at Emory University Hospital. Now at least we could see each other and speak through the intercom.

Kent still in isolation but feeling better, catching up on calls and texts.

Kent's
Man Cave

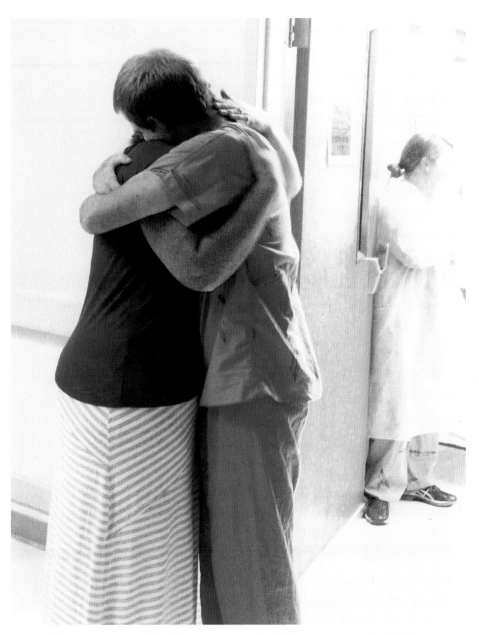

Kent stepping out of isolation on August 20, 2014, and experiencing his first
human contact in a month. We'll never forget this embrace.

Saying good-bye to the staff at Emory University Hospital—
no personal protective equipment!

Meeting with President Barack Obama in the Oval Office, September 16, 2014.

the group Jars of Clay singing popular hymns. After Kent boarded the plane, there was a long delay, and he sat there and listened to Jars of Clay singing "I Need Thee Every Hour" on repeat.

Hearing that song over and over comforted Kent after the loss of his grand-father. Like for me while sitting in the mesquite tree, a song became his prayer in a time of sorrow . . . and the hymn has remained so meaningful to him.

After Ruby was born in 2009, he sang that hymn to her every night as we tried to get her to fall asleep. I think Kent's favorite part was,

I need Thee every hour, in joy or pain;
Come quickly and abide, or life is in vain.

I need Thee, O I need Thee;
Every hour I need Thee;
O bless me now, my Savior!
I come to Thee.[12]

Ruby heard that song so much that when she was eighteen months old, we used a phone to video her singing the song by herself. You'd have to know how to translate baby talk to understand her, but it's obvious she knew every word.

Praying and singing those hymns did not make my hurt go away. As much as I would like to, I can't claim that I felt the same peace as Kent said he was feeling. I thought my husband was going to die. I was in pain. I was afraid. Through those hymns, though, I was able to connect with God in a meaningful way when I couldn't find my own words to pray.

During difficult times, Kent and I had learned to reflect on what God had done in our lives and the calling that he had given us, because doing so put every-thing into perspective. We'd heard older missionaries say that the work of mis-sions is not safe. There are no promises that we will always be free of danger. The next day is never guaranteed. However, the missionaries could speak from their experiences and assure us of this: the safest place that we can be is in the center of God's will.

In C. S. Lewis's children's fiction classic *The Lion, the Witch and the Wardrobe,* four children meet Mr. and Mrs. Beaver in the magical kingdom of Narnia. The beavers describe for the children the great lion Aslan, whom Lewis used in the story to represent Jesus.

Susan, one of the children, anticipates that she would be rather nervous about meeting a lion, and Mrs. Beaver agrees that she will be.

"Then he isn't safe?" young Lucy asks.

Mr. Beaver responds, "Safe? Don't you hear what Mrs. Beaver tells you? Who said anything about safe? 'Course he isn't safe. But he's good. He's the King, I tell you."[13]

We knew that the life we had chosen as missionaries was not safe as the world measures safety. But we were confident that God had called us to this work, and that was all the security we needed. As Lucy did with Aslan the lion, we believe that God *is* good.

Sitting in that mesquite tree, hurting and afraid of what my future might hold yet placing my trust in him, I felt surrounded by God's goodness.

"Daddy Is Sick"

I returned to the house for dinner. The guests had all arrived, and my dad had informed them about Kent's test results. I was greeted by a round of hugs when I walked in. It was a glum birthday party for Kevin.

I didn't tell the kids that Kent had Ebola. They were five and three at the time. They knew about Ebola and that a lot of people in Liberia had been dying because of it. They knew that Ebola was the reason we had to stop going to market and why the ELWA beach had been closed to the public.

"Daddy is sick," I told Ruby and Stephen. "We are all just worried about Daddy, and we need to remember to pray for him as often as we can think of it."

It wasn't long until those at the house started reading about Kent on social media. Samaritan's Purse had issued a news release about Kent's having Ebola in a strategic move to get ahead of the news story. Otherwise, with all the organizations involved in the situation in Liberia, rumors and leaks would have been the first reports, and the likelihood of those being accurate was slim. SP smartly wanted to control what was being initially reported. Still, though, we received word from family in Alaska who said they'd heard reports that Kent had died.

Fully aware now that the world was learning of Kent's illness, I immediately switched into a businesslike mode.

I need to check Kent's Facebook and see what his privacy settings are.

I logged in with Kent's password and saw that he already had received dozens of friend requests. Many seemed to be reporters. I went through the requests and declined all of them, then changed Kent's settings from public to private.

I texted Kent to tell him that SP had issued a news release and asked if I should send an e-mail letter to all our supporters. Kent said that would be a good idea. Before I wrote the letter, I also learned on a phone call with Kent that Nancy Writebol had tested positive for Ebola in addition to malaria.

Dear Friends,

It is with heavy hearts we write tonight. Kent has contracted the dreaded Ebola Virus Disease. He has been quarantined in our home in Liberia. Amber and the children traveled to Texas several days before Kent became ill. The Lord has spared us that. (Since one is only contagious for the disease when he/she is symptomatic, we feel confident that we were not exposed to the virus.) In addition, our good friend and fellow missionary, Nancy, has also tested positive for the virus and is being treated in her home.

We need your prayers. Please pray for Kent's and Nancy's complete healing.

Please pray for comfort and peace for Amber, Ruby, and Stephen, and for all our family.

Please pray for the other health-care workers at the Case Management Center to have peace about working, even while seeing their coworkers become sick.

Pray for God to be glorified in it all, and for Satan to not use this crisis for his own gain.

∾

I had mixed feelings Saturday night. I wanted so badly to be in Monrovia with Kent. Since I am a nurse, I naturally want to nurture others when they are sick— and this was especially true with the man I love so much. I had some good home-made chicken broth in our freezer, and I wanted to go home and warm that up for Kent, like that would cure him. I just wanted to be there with him. I felt so helpless.

But then I also was thankful that we weren't there. If the kids and I had been with Kent, we would have been exposed to the virus. Because we had flown out three days ahead of when Kent first became ill, I knew there was no danger to the three of us. I was thankful to be with our kids. I knew God could heal Kent, but I did not know if we would ever be a family of four again.

When I tucked the kids into bed, Stephen prayed, "Please help Daddy to be safe and sound and snuggled to bed. Amen."

Alone at the end of a day I'll never forget, I opened my journal and stared at the blank page. What could I really say? I wrote only three words, with long spaces in between:

Kent   has   Ebola

Kent

I felt a very real sense of peace that entire day. I have no explanation other than it was a gift from God. Even up until when Lance and John told me the test result, I didn't think I had Ebola, even though the evidence was pointing more in that direction. Perhaps I had adapted to Liberian culture and did not want to speak negatively by admitting I probably had the disease.

Regardless, I had been told that I had what amounted to a death sentence and my response was, "What are we going to do?"

Unbeknownst to me, while John had stepped out of my bedroom so I could call Amber and my parents, he went into another room and prayed for me. He stayed with me long into the night.

11

Bad News, Bad Signs

Kent

J ohn Fankhauser did not need more stress. He was already taking care of me and tending to his seemingly endless duties at the hospital. But more stress is what he got when he found out Nancy also had Ebola.

John's wife, Beth, had delivered chicken-noodle soup to Nancy and visited with her for an hour when Nancy was known to have malaria. Nancy's subsequent diagnosis of Ebola made Beth a contact and required that she be isolated.

John decided that if Beth had contracted Ebola, she would be more comfortable being treated in their home, so John and their two teenage daughters, Bethany and Bekah, started moving out of their home late Saturday night.

They finished moving around 3 a.m., and I sent him an update a few minutes later to report that I had taken my medicine, my temperature was 101.8, I was feeling fine, and I would be going back to sleep.

John asked if I would be okay with him getting some sleep, then coming to check on me at 6 a.m. When John came, I was having pain and diarrhea. He gave me two doses of morphine in addition to fluids, my other medicines, and vitamins.

Two or three times a day, John reassured me that I would survive: "There's just something about you," he'd say. "You look like you are going to make it."

The statistics for Ebola suggested differently, but every time John encouraged me with those words, I chose to believe him.

Overnight Saturday and into Sunday morning, I received text messages of support from numerous friends.

Scott Parker told me, "As you know, we are praying for you. I know it has been a big spiritual battle for months since your arrival, and we continue to battle with you in the spiritual realm. I hope it goes without saying, but please call any hour, day or night, if it is of any benefit to you. Love you, man. For my reading this morning: 'I have told you all this so that you may have peace in me. Here on earth you will have many trials and sorrows. But take heart, because I have overcome the world.'"[14]

"Amen," I responded.

Scott Bedichek, a periodontist friend from our church, had sent me a text Saturday night that I responded to Sunday morning. He answered, "If your goal by moving to Liberia was to bring people to Christ, well done. The church has been in prayer all through the night. People are fasting today. Countless people are calling on his name. I will let you rest, but I wanted to let you know all the Christians I know, and even those who don't truly know God, are in prayer."

My mom texted me as she and my dad were arriving at their church. "The whole world is praying for you. God hears. My phone is in my hand. You can call me anytime. I love you."

Eric Buller sent me a text that made me laugh. "Praying for you, brother. I love you. Hope that wasn't too awkward."

"Thanks, brother," I told him. "Love you too."

Randy Harris called me early that afternoon, which was prior to church time in Fort Worth. My brother Kerry had called Randy after my test result. I have since asked Kerry why he called Randy, because he seemed like such a random person for Kerry to call.

"Brother," he told me, "I called him because I didn't know what to do for you. You were in Liberia dying of Ebola, and I had no way to help you. But I knew that

Randy had been a mentor of sorts to you, and I thought maybe he could minister to you in a way that I wasn't able to."

I answered Randy's call.

"I don't know what to say," he told me. "It took me ten minutes to pick myself up off the floor, and I don't know what to say to you. I'm so sorry."

It was Randy who had preached on Romans 8:28 at our church the previous Sunday, and he would be speaking there again that day on the topic "Being Transformed by Prayer."

"Do you have a message for your church family?" he asked.

I told Randy, "Tell them, 'Thank you for praying for me,' and that I just want God to be glorified in my life or in my death. I keep thinking about Shadrach, Meshach, and Abednego facing death in the fiery furnace. They told the king that they knew their God could deliver them. But even if he didn't, they would still be faithful to him and would not bow down to the king's idol.[15]

"I know that God can save me. I know he can. But even if he doesn't, I don't want to deny him. I want to be faithful."

Amber

I decided not to go to church Sunday morning, and my parents stayed home with me. Kent called me after talking with Randy and told me what he had shared about Shadrach, Meshach, and Abednego. I was so proud of Kent. I knew that the peace he had was a gift from God, and I knew that Kent would have peace whether he lived or died.

My parents were scheduled to host a small-group meeting in their home later that day, but they canceled that because I wasn't ready to be around a bunch of people who would be asking about Kent.

My sister Anne came home from church and told us that it was announced that Kent was sick with Ebola and that our family had been quarantined. We told Dad that he needed to get with the church leaders right away and correct that misinformation.

My friend Tammy texted to ask if she could deliver us bread and some of her homemade jams. I told her to come on over. Tammy told us more about the quarantine announcement, and Dad sent an e-mail to all the church members clarifying that we were not under quarantine.

Tammy arrived and was good company while helping me figure out how to privatize the blog I had been keeping. With news continuing to spread, I wanted to keep things as private as possible for all of us. It was overwhelming enough living with the possibility that Kent could die without my ever being able to see or touch him again.

Extra Doses of Bad News

Kent

Samaritan's Purse leadership held a conference call from its North Carolina headquarters with the team on the ground in Liberia. Ken Isaacs, SP's vice president of program and government relations, asked John Fankhauser what was needed to save my life. John listed several items and emphasized the need for me to receive a higher level of care. Until that could happen, John requested that he be allowed to talk on a regular basis to a doctor with ICU skills, which he began doing the next day.

John came by in the afternoon. With word now out about my condition, it no longer was necessary for those coming to see me to have to step inside my house to put on their PPE. The front porch became the new place to suit up.

After checking on me, John left.

I received another text from Scott Parker that afternoon. He said he hated to bother me about this, but he was torn about how to respond to the media. "The stories are running everywhere, as you know, and I just want to respond in a way you are comfortable with. I am sure this is the least of your concerns. Thousands are praying. Millions are hearing about Jesus and about Ebola. We are praying. God will be glorified."

"Hey, man," I wrote back. "I am not sure I understand your question. Have you been contacted by media outlets?"

Scott replied that after national media had reported that Nancy and I had Ebola, he had begun hearing from local TV stations and newspapers asking him to comment as a representative of our church. "They want to run stories about you like there have been on all the big outlets. I don't know if I should speak to the reporters or decline. And if I do speak to them, what would you want said? My inclination is to say that, 'Kent loves God and loves people. We are praying fervently for Kent's recovery and for God to be glorified'—or something like that. News on the Internet says you are stable and working on your laptop. Any improvement?"

"My condition waxes and wanes," I answered. "Had a high fever midday, but lower tonight. Feeling a little better but having more diarrhea. I think it is okay for you to speak to them, and what you said sounds fine. David McRay called me; he said JPS is having a press conference tomorrow and he is going to be the spokesperson, so maybe you could just direct them to that conference."

A little before 6 p.m., I sent John a quick text: "I need you."

This is another one of those times for which I have little recall, but John has told me that I had summoned him because I was feeling really anxious more than anything else. I do remember the feeling of anxiety from being alone, but I do not remember that dominating me.

There were times when I would wake up alone and too weak to get out of bed. I would feel anxious and say aloud, "Who's there? Is there anybody in here?" And no one was there to answer. Or I would really need someone to come to our house, and it would take them an hour or two to get there. I knew our staff was being stretched too thin and my colleagues were providing me the absolute best care they could. John alone was probably spending ten hours a day with me, wearing full PPE.

Just the day before, four patients in our hospital had died from Ebola in a span of two hours. Two of them had been bleeding profusely, which increased the risk of contamination through the blood and body fluids. The deaths were an added stress on the team, not to mention the trauma of dealing with such graphic suffering.

One of the deceased was Dr. Samuel Brisbane, a well-respected and high-profile doctor. Dr. Brisbane was the first Liberian doctor to die during the outbreak. His death added an extra political dimension to the crisis, while exacerbating heightened emotions.

The Liberian medical community had already been hurt by the disproportionate number of local health-care workers who had died. We foreigners had worked alongside them as colleagues, but those who died were their friends—people they had studied and worked with, often for years. They had remained resolute in the battle against Ebola, but the crushing burden of fighting a killer disease while under-resourced was taking its toll.

Patients were arriving at our treatment unit, where no beds were available, and phone calls were coming in to alert my colleagues that more suspected Ebola patients were on the way. Our morgue had run out of room because the Ministry of Health burial team could not keep up with the workload.

And on top of that, Saturday night, the missionaries were gathered to be told that two of their own—Nancy and I—had Ebola.

Everyone was going above and beyond to help—sacrificially caring for me. But there were those times, like that Sunday evening, when I felt so alone, and I hated that feeling.

John gave me a dose of morphine as well as the artesunate and vitamins, then sat next to the bed for a while to keep me company.

DISCUSSING OPTIONS

At some point that Sunday evening, while John was seated at my bedside, I was sitting up in bed with my laptop open when Lance appeared outside my bedroom window with Dr. Lisa Hensley. Lisa was a virologist from Maryland who worked for the National Institute of Allergy and Infectious Diseases (NIAID). One of the world's top researchers of infectious diseases, she had been studying Ebola in the United States for well over a decade and at the time was working in the Liberian lab that processed Ebola tests.

To this day, the last picture on my cell phone from Liberia was of me with Lisa and Dr. Randy Schoepp, chief of diagnostics with US Army Medical Research Institute of Infectious Diseases (USAMRIID). They, and another expert, had visited ELWA on July 22, the day before I awoke feeling not so great, to offer their help with our laboratory response.

Five days later, Lisa was back to offer me a vastly different type of help.

Lance had reached out to Lisa for information concerning therapy options for Nancy and me, and she offered to come back to ELWA and meet with us in person.

Lisa asked if I had knowledge of experimental treatment options for Ebola. I told her that I had been looking into them online during my stronger moments. The way I remember it, Lisa said there were three significant novel drugs for Ebola. She was extremely knowledgeable and able to offer detailed explanations of each.

The first drug was a vaccine, which would not help me because I was already sick. The second was a cocktail of antibodies that targeted the Ebola virus. The third was a drug that aimed to stop the virus from replicating.

Lisa said the third drug had shown great promise in early trials, but the trials had to be stopped because researchers noticed side effects that included increased inflammation. Ebola results in harmful inflammation within the body, caused by the immune system's attempt to defeat the virus. So the risk of further increasing inflammation in Ebola patients was too great, as it could prove fatal.

The antibodies, Lisa told me, had yet to be given to a human. About eighteen monkeys had been treated with the drug, and all had lived. Most encouraging, the monkeys had been given the serum at various times during the course of the illness, even up to the point where researchers knew the animals were near death. No other treatment that had been in trial had been able to save a monkey in the latest stages, but this drug had a 100 percent success rate.

Because the drug had not been administered to a human, there was no way of knowing whether it was safe. The serum was derived from a mouse antibody and grown in tobacco plants. It is a type of monoclonal antibody. I knew that monoclonal antibodies were engineered in laboratories to imitate antibodies naturally produced as part of the body's immune system. That type of treatment had been employed to treat other conditions, and as far as I knew they were generally considered to be safe.

Lisa said she believed that there were one or two courses of the antibodies in West Africa. She and Lance were having their own discussions, and they seemed to believe that the antibodies were the best bet for helping me.

"If the antibodies are available, I would be willing to receive them," I said. "I would be the guinea pig."

Lisa was equally impressive and helpful. Before she left my window, she told Lance that she would be willing to donate a unit of blood if I began hemorrhaging.

John stayed at my house until midnight, then he came into my room, said "Good night," and left to face his own personal uncertainty—the apartment he and his daughters had moved into while his wife was isolated.

Problems in the Mirror

At 5 a.m. Monday, I awoke to three episodes of large black watery stools in a period of fifteen minutes.

I alerted John by text.

"On my way," he responded.

The medical term for what I had is *melena*. The black color comes from broken-down, digested blood products. That meant there was bleeding somewhere in my gastrointestinal tract.

One problem with being a doctor who had treated Ebola patients was that I knew all the symptoms, and I could speculate in my mind which symptom might appear next. The one Monday morning was new and disturbing. When a patient with Ebola develops GI bleeding, the mortality rate rises dramatically.

Within an hour John was at my house to give me a unit of blood from the hospital's blood bank. I went into the bathroom and almost fainted. John had to dash into the bathroom and hold me up.

I also developed a petechial rash: small red spots from my chest out to my arms. Their appearance meant blood vessels had broken in those areas. Over the next couple of days, the rash would progress until the spots coalesced into a generalized, large red erythematous rash from head to toe. My skin felt thick, and each time I went into the bathroom, I pulled down my shirt from my neck and looked into the mirror. My skin was bright red.

From the first day of illness, I had looked at my eyes in the mirror several times a day. Red, bloodshot eyes were one of the telltale signs of Ebola. It seemed like for every suspected patient we saw, if her eyes were red, we could predict her outcome: death. For the first time, my eyes were bloodshot red.

Early that afternoon, John measured my temperature at 104.3 and my heart rate at 120 beats per minute. Later in the day, after John had left, my temperature edged up to 104.5.

I talked with my cousin Stephen—Big Stephen we called him, because our little Stephen is his namesake. "I'm really scared," Stephen remembers me saying.

Stephen told me that he was scared for me too.

Amber

My parents had taken vacation time to prepare for the wedding, and the foster kids weren't with us in the home. On Monday, my dad reported to his supervisor that the kids and I were staying in their home, and that Kent had tested positive for Ebola over the weekend.

That started a series of conversations between Dad's bosses and the Texas state licensing department and state health department. Beginning that day, the kids and I were required to take our temperatures four times per day, with two readings each time. We had to keep a log, but I couldn't sign it myself. Each temperature reading had to be verified by the signatures of two witnesses.

Then one of the state agencies came back to us and said it would be better if the kids and I looked for somewhere else to stay, away from the foster home.

My mom texted a few close friends asking if anyone knew of a place we could move to. One friend answered right away with a suggestion.

I was stressed about moving out of my parents' home right in the middle of worrying about Kent's health. This was the only house in Abilene my kids knew, and Mom and Dad had a really wonderful golden retriever that had been therapeutic for Ruby and Stephen, and me too.

Although I understood the state agency's fear about us, it was an overreaction. We had left Liberia three whole days before Kent got sick, and it wasn't necessary to force us to move. It was not just in Abilene. All across the country, people were nervous about Ebola.

∾

Ruby asked me that day, "Why is everybody so sad?"

"We're worried for Daddy," I said. "He is sick in Liberia."

12

The Humiliation of Ebola

Kent

Tuesday was a bad day for a variety of reasons.

At 4 a.m., I threw up. My vomit was bloody.

"I just vomited about 50 cc of maroon-colored emesis," I texted John.

"Still nauseated?" he asked.

"No," I answered.

"Will get Alex to donate early in the morning. I will call them at 6 a.m. Text me if you have any more."

Alex was Eric and Pam Buller's sixteen-year-old daughter, and she had been identified as a potential donor if I needed blood. All four of the Buller teenagers wanted to donate, but Alex and I were a blood-type match.

A fresh blood transfusion was preferred over one from the blood bank. Platelets and clotting factors diminish over time, and while frozen blood from the bank would be good for replenishing my supply of red blood cells, it would not help me stop bleeding. With Ebola, the blood stops clotting, and without a transfusion containing someone else's platelets and clotting factors, the bleeding would continue.

John was at my house with a unit of blood from Alex before 6 a.m. After texting me, he had changed his mind and contacted the Bullers right away to have Alex go to the hospital to donate. Thanks to Alex, I received my second transfusion.

I heard from Amber via text in the morning, sharing with me another hymn that had been playing in her mind.

"Good morning, my love," I responded. "Had a pretty rough night."

"Honey, I have not stopped praying for you," Amber wrote. "You are my sunshine. I hope you can rest now, but call me when you can. Jamie [her sister-in-law] was in labor last night. How are you, love?"

I was too tired and weak to answer her.

Supportive messages continued to come in through texts.

Scott Parker told me, "Hey, brother. I talked to your dad briefly and understand things are tough. Words fail me, but Psalm 46:1 is on my heart: 'God is our refuge and strength, an ever-present help in trouble.' Praying for courage, faith, peace, encouragement, and complete healing, and above all that God would be glorified through your life, that his Kingdom may come and his will be done on earth as it is in heaven. I had breakfast with Johny and Philip this morning. We prayed that together and continue to petition the Lord."

My brother Kerry texted me midmorning and asked if I felt up to talking.

"Not right now. Sorry," I texted back.

"I love you," he said.

"I love you too. Please pray for my diarrhea to stop. It is getting a lot worse."

"Okay," my brother said. "You are not alone. We so wish we could be there with you right now. You will make it through and recover. Randy Harris told me you talked with him about Daniel's friends. I am praying God will encourage you like he did the boys while they were in the furnace. He loves you."

Another brother, Kevin, also texted me that day: "I love you. I am praying your diarrhea subsides and God holds you in his hand."

I had been told that thousands of people, if not more, were praying for me around the world. But that one prayer by Kevin really got to me. Kevin was not a praying man. But he became one.

A NEW HOME

Amber

Ruby, Stephen, and I packed up Tuesday morning and moved to our new place, which turned out to be a true gift for us.

We stayed in a guest house on a lake just a few miles from where my parents lived. The guest house was behind the main house and surrounded by a privacy fence. Nobody knew we were there except for family, the friend who had arranged it, and the homeowners.

We were so well provided for there. Not only was the house on a lake, but there was also a swimming pool and the owners had lots of kids' things there for Ruby and Stephen to enjoy. The guest house had plenty of room and allowed us to be alone with family. The owners also gave me their WiFi password and let me come into the back of their house where I could get a better signal for communicating with Kent.

Mary Elizabeth Jameson and Melissa Strickland from Samaritan's Purse flew to Abilene that day. Mary Elizabeth managed the post-residency program, and Melissa was the editorial director at Samaritan's Purse. They didn't ask if I wanted them to come; they knew I needed their help.

Mary Elizabeth just wanted to sit with me during my trial and help in whatever ways she could. Melissa came on behalf of SP to help us manage the media. Newscasters and reporters had found out the cell numbers of some of my siblings and were calling them—even showing up at their homes. Melissa took over communicating with the media so that we could take care of what was most important—each other and praying for Kent's healing.

Mary Elizabeth went shopping for me and bought me some clothes since I'd packed for Texas intending to stay only a few weeks. She also watched the kids, feeding them and entertaining them. I had a lot of help keeping life as normal as possible. My friend Tammy took Ruby and Stephen to the zoo one day. They had a crew of uncles and aunts around them too, taking them swimming and fishing and to try on wedding clothes.

Evacuation Falls Through

Kent

Samaritan's Purse had been working feverishly to have me evacuated to another country where I could receive the more advanced care John had advised that I needed. Hospitals in Brussels, Belgium, and Geneva, Switzerland, were the most likely locations, because MSF had a policy whereby if any of their workers were exposed to Ebola during an outbreak, they could be sent to those places to be monitored.

Just a week earlier, Lance and I had met with a senior MSF official in Liberia about that contingency plan. But as far as I knew, no plan covered someone who already had Ebola. This was a different ballgame altogether.

There had been issues with securing a plane to fly me out of Liberia. SP had emergency medical-evacuation insurance, but the insurance company balked upon learning that the person needing evacuation was a patient with Ebola.

Samaritan's Purse began to turn to government agencies and the military for help. Ken Isaacs used his contacts in the State Department to plead my case.

Dr. William Walters, the director of operational medicine at the State Department, had just completed the arrangements for the evacuation of another US citizen from some faraway place. Now he was asked about the possibility of evacuating an American doctor sick with Ebola. Dr. Walters searched my name on the Internet, and the first thing he came across was a picture of Amber and me with Ruby and Stephen. Something about seeing our family touched his heart, and he resolved to do what he could to have me evacuated.

Dr. Walters contacted Dent Thompson, COO and senior vice president of US-based Phoenix Air, which had a contract with the State Department. The two had worked together on previous projects.

"You remember that containment unit you guys used to have? Does it still work?" Dr. Walters asked.

"I think it does," Thompson said. "But we've never used it."

The CDC had developed the Airborne Biomedical Containment Systems (ABCS) in 2008 for evacuating any CDC employee in case of an exposure or infection during a public-health crisis, such as the SARS outbreak of 2002–03. But there had never been an occasion to use the ABCS.

Dr. Walters's next question knocked Thompson back on his heels.

"Will it work for Ebola?"

"You better send your experts down here and let us figure this out together," Dent told him.

In a matter of three days, the experts concluded that the system was sufficient for transporting an Ebola patient.

The hospitals in Brussels and Geneva had agreed to take me in as a patient. But on Tuesday I found out that evacuation to Europe was a no-go. Countries in both North Africa and Europe had refused to grant clearance for a plane with me on board to fly through their air space. If our plane needed to make an emergency landing or crashed, they did not want someone carrying Ebola on the ground.

Also that day, we received word that Samaritan's Purse workers near Foya had been attacked. The workers were trying to help investigate reported suspicious deaths in a more rural area when their SUVs were ambushed by a machete-and-stick-wielding mob intent on keeping the Ebola team out of their village. The SUVs were smashed and windows broken. The workers survived, but some were badly beaten.

Those were our teammates, and it was frightening that good people who were trying to help were having their lives endangered.

There was one bit of good news. I heard from Gebah, the fourteen-year-old who was our lone Ebola survivor. He had called me from time to time after leaving the hospital and happened to call me that day.

"How are you doing, Dr. Brantly?" he asked.

"Well, Gebah, you know that Ebola virus you had? Well, I have it now, and I am really sick."

Gebah told me that he and his family would be praying for me and that he wanted to help me. "I think I need to talk to your uncle," I told him. "Could I talk to your uncle sometime?"

Gebah said he would have his uncle call me.

My phone rang soon after. I explained to Gebah's uncle that I was sick with Ebola and bleeding on the inside. My doctors thought that Gebah's blood would be better for me than anyone else's because his immune system had beaten Ebola. I told the uncle that if Gebah's blood type matched mine, he could help me by donating blood.

The uncle said that he had already left his home for a celebration on the last night of Ramadan, but that he would bring Gebah to the hospital the next day to donate blood.

I texted John to let him know that Gebah's uncle would be calling him to arrange the donation.

Then the emotional roller coaster started back down.

Dr. Debbie and Kathy Mazzella, one of our nurses, came to visit me that evening. They informed me that when John had left my house that morning, he wasn't feeling well and had a fever. He had to go into quarantine for seventy-two hours before being tested for Ebola. I was scared and heartbroken, thinking that John could also have Ebola, but I was also upset with him for not taking better care of himself.

Now who is going to take care of me? I wondered.

While Debbie and Kathy were at my house, Amber and I chatted via text again, with me telling her that I was feeling better and that Lance had said he would soon be meeting the Department of Defense to inquire whether evacuation remained a possibility.

Amber asked me to have Debbie or Kathy get for me our wedding photo album and a photo album from my parents' fiftieth wedding anniversary. She wanted me to keep the albums on my bed so I could have them close by to look at.

I tried to FaceTime Amber a little later that night, but she did not answer. I texted to let her I know I was trying to reach her.

"I love you so much, baby. Hang on," she told me.

Amber

The news that Kent would not be evacuated to Brussels was crushing, because I had initially been told that he would be flying out that day. That was before all necessary air-space clearances had come in, though. So when I was told that Kent would not fly to Belgium, a sense of doom set in because, to me, Kent's only hope for survival was treatment in a more modern medical facility.

I tried to sound strong when I talked with Kent because I didn't want him to worry about me and the kids. He didn't know the extent of the media coverage and how my brothers and sisters were being hounded. He didn't know that we had been kicked out of my parents' house. I told him that we had moved to a new place and turned my phone around to show him a panorama of the backyard.

"Wait—whose house are you at? Is that the Griggses' house?" he asked.

I told him it was.

"I have been there. I swam in that pool," he said. "We had a social-club activity there when I was in college."

At least he knew exactly where we were, and it seemed to comfort him that we were perfectly safe and happy there.

Later that evening, I was sitting in our hosts' office using their Internet with my parents in the room. I received a call from Kent and stood to answer it. My dad came over to me to listen.

Kent told me about the workers who had been attacked, and I tried to sound upbeat for him.

After we ended the call, I collapsed into my chair and exclaimed to my dad, "This is horrible! This is horrible! It is absolute chaos!"

Dad held me, like he was so good at doing, and Mom knelt beside us and leaned against me.

In that moment, Mom's phone dinged with a text photo announcing Samuel's birth.

I almost lost it. It was just too much emotion for me to handle. I had spent the day on my own emotional roller coaster, because one minute I was receiving the bad news about Kent's evacuation and another I was hearing that Geoff and

Jamie's long-awaited first baby had been born. When I saw the pictures of my new nephew, all I could think was, *The Lord gives, and the Lord takes away. He is giving us Samuel, and he is taking away Kent.* I just knew that was the case.

Samuel was born in a town a two-and-a-half-hour drive away, and my parents told Geoff they didn't think we would be able to make it down that night. They asked him if they could visit the next day.

Anticipation of this baby being born had been a big reason Kent and I decided to make this trip. The wedding and the birth were two huge family events, and we decided that we would come back to Texas because both were happening close together.

And now the baby had been born, the wedding was only four days away, I was in Abilene with the kids, and Kent was six thousand miles away in Liberia, getting sicker and needing blood transfusions while our efforts there seemed to be all for nothing.

GEBAH'S GIFT

Kent

John had arranged for Gebah to come to the hospital the next day to give blood for me. But John had to go into quarantine, and Gebah's uncle called him Wednesday morning to say there was no one at the hospital who could help him. John called the head of the lab and asked him to go draw blood from Gebah. An hour later, Gebah's uncle called John again and said, "We are leaving. They told us the boy is too little. He can't give blood for an adult."

"No, please don't leave," John pleaded, then he called Dr. Debbie to ask her to step in and help.

Debbie explained the situation to the head of the lab, who checked Gebah's blood type to see if it was a match for me. Then the uncle and Debbie prayed together. It turned out that Gebah's blood was a perfect match. Gebah donated a unit of blood, and Debbie brought it directly to my house and started my third transfusion in as many days.

The IV in my right arm was beginning to slow down, and Debbie needed to start a new IV so the blood would run better. She climbed across the other side of the bed and leaned over on her knees and elbows to place an IV in my left arm.

Debbie said, "I am so sorry. I'm so sorry. You shouldn't have to do this to your friend. I shouldn't have to stick my friend with a needle."

Her words struck me hard. My friends were coming in to take care of me and even strong, stoic Dr. Debbie was saying, "This is not right. I shouldn't have to do this to a friend."

Yet I was so thankful that friends were taking care of me, that I was being cared for by people who I knew loved me. I had been working with John and Debbie for nine months, and Lance for about a month. Some of the nurses were new and had arrived after I had become sick. But they were coming in and taking care of me just like those I had worked with for months.

I have described Ebola as humiliating for patients. I experienced that humiliation firsthand when I reached the point that I could not control my diarrhea and could not get up to go to the bathroom. Someone would be in the bedroom with me, taking care of me, and I would say, "I'm about to go. I can't stop it. I'm sorry." They had to clean me up and throw away the waste. At some point they started putting adult diapers on me. I had to tell them when I had diarrhea in my diaper and let them change my diaper for me.

It was hard to ask, "Can you change my diaper for me?"

But as hard as that was for me, it must have been only a fraction of the emotional weight carried by my friends caring for me.

When you are cleaning up vomit or changing a diaper for a patient, there is generally a level of emotional distance. You're just cleaning up for someone. But when that patient is your friend whom you think is probably going to die, it is much more difficult. That does not even take into account the risk of being exposed to Ebola through all those body fluids. The sicker I got, the riskier it became to care for me. But my friends did it, and they did it well. They went out of their way to take care of me while still having to do their work at the hospital.

My sister Krista had been texting me, and on Wednesday she sent me the entire text of Psalm 41, which begins with these verses:

Blessed are those who have regard for the weak;
 the LORD delivers them in times of trouble.
The LORD protects and preserves them—
 they are counted among the blessed in the land—
 he does not give them over to the desire of their foes.
The LORD sustains them on their sickbed
 and restores them from their bed of illness.

13

The Day Kent Almost Died

Amber

Each time I talked with Kent, I could tell he was feeling worse. He even admitted that a few times. Kent hadn't had the energy to have long conversations to begin with. But our talks were growing shorter, maybe from seven to ten minutes down to three or four minutes at a time. At the end of the conversation, it seemed like talking to me had drained all his energy.

When we FaceTimed, it hurt to see how much his health had deteriorated. Whereas before he had sat up in bed with the computer on his lap when he talked to me, he now was lying down, with the computer propped up beside him, like it had taken all his strength just to open the screen. Also, his eyes appeared to be getting deeper as his face became more swollen.

Each time we FaceTimed I took a screenshot of him, just in case that turned out to be the last time I saw him alive.

With our talks now so short, I didn't want to spend most of our time asking Kent for medical updates. I wanted to save as much time as possible for personal things, like telling him I loved him and filling him in on what the kids were doing. I had a prepaid GoPhone and didn't have an international plan, so I wasn't able to just call someone in Liberia and ask about Kent. I had been receiving updates mostly from Lance Plyler and, occasionally, John Fankhauser. I could e-mail Eric Buller, our next-door neighbor, but he could only relay what he had been told, because he was not in the house with Kent.

Unfortunately, late in the day Wednesday, Lance met the redhead portion of my personality. The stress of the week had taken its toll on me. A good night's sleep no longer seemed possible. Both my mom and I would wake up in the middle of the night and check the time. If it was around 3 or 4 a.m., it would be 8 or 9 a.m. in Monrovia, and someone there would have already gone to the house for the morning check on Kent. We would look at our phones for text messages and any general news on Facebook to see if Kent had survived the night.

I couldn't be with Kent, so I wanted to know every minute how he was doing.

"Look," I told Lance, "I am sitting here on pins and needles all day with no word from you on Kent's condition. I just need a phone call. I need a phone call every day."

"Oh, okay," Lance calmly responded. "Yes, I can do that."

Poor guy. He was working his tail off, dealing not only with the stress of managing the entire response to the outbreak, but also of having two US workers stricken with Ebola.

Lance was supposed to have left Liberia on Monday. He had arrived in June to help take over management of the Ebola treatment unit in Foya, and his responsibilities had increased during his weeks there. The original plan called for Dr. Linda Mobula to arrive on Sunday, spend time orienting with Lance, then Lance would leave Monday and Linda would take his place as manager of the disaster response team. But with everything falling apart, Lance couldn't leave.

Receiving updates about Kent was one area—among several—where Melissa from Samaritan's Purse stepped in and provided so much help. She began to maintain contact with Ken Isaacs, who was getting regular updates from Lance, and I could keep up better with Kent through them without taking anyone in Liberia away from their responsibilities.

Prayers from Around the World

Kent sounded terrible when he called me on Thursday. It was late afternoon in Liberia, and Kent couldn't recall anyone having been with him for the past few hours. His breathing was heavy, and he could barely hold a conversation. He didn't seem very lucid to me. The call was shorter than most because he was so weak.

As I ended the call with Kent, I promptly turned to Melissa Strickland.

"He is all alone. They have to get someone over there right now. He is all alone, and he is not okay. If he tries to get up to go to the bathroom and faints, there is no one there that is going to check on him for hours."

Melissa called Ken Isaacs, who got in touch with Lance in Monrovia. Then Ken called me to let me know Lance was on his way to the house.

"Just calm down and be strong," Ken tried to reassure me. "He is okay."

."I don't want to calm down," I said. "Kent is alone, and he is dying alone. That is not okay with me."

In that condition, Kent needed someone with him constantly. But I knew that they didn't have the manpower to provide that.

Before someone could get suited up and go in to be with Kent, Lance hurried over to the house and looked through the bedroom window. Then he called me.

Because our little cabana had become the prewedding gathering place for family, I stepped into the bathroom and shut the door so I could hear Lance better.

"Kent is not doing well," he told me. "You need to pray right now. Hard. Like you have never prayed before."

I walked back into the living room.

"What's the word?" someone asked. I'm not sure who asked.

"We just have to pray," I said. "We just have to pray right now."

My mom started asking questions.

"What is it? What's wrong? What's going on?"

"I don't know. Just pray."

"Should I take the kids—"

"Just pray! Just pray!"

I dropped to my knees behind the couch. Everyone circled around me and began praying, some out loud, some silently.

Ruby sat on my lap, and I hugged her tight to me.

Mary Elizabeth from Samaritan's Purse, who had gone to pick up some chicken nuggets for the kids, walked in the door and sensed a crisis. She looked around the room and didn't even ask a question. She dropped the food onto the table, grabbed the kids, and said, "Let's go play outside."

Texts from inside our room were going out, asking people to pray. People from our church began praying immediately.

Scott Parker walked out of a meeting at work to sit in his car and pray. At SP's headquarters in North Carolina, word of Kent's condition was delivered during a staff meeting. They stopped the meeting and began praying. Everyone at SP prayed.

When we met Franklin Graham for the first time, he told us that in the moment when he received our urgent prayer request, he laid on his office floor for an hour interceding for Kent, pleading for the Lord to spare his life along with all the people in Liberia.

We've also heard from people who knew nothing of Kent's condition but felt at that time an urge to pray for him. People all over the world, literally, were praying for him, and he needed those prayers.

Kent

Thursday was the day I thought I would die.

I was weaker, had no control of my bowels, and was having frequent diarrhea. Breathing had become progressively more difficult throughout the day. My body could not win that fight. I thought I was going to die of respiratory failure that night.

There were only a few courses of the experimental drug in the world. One had arrived on the ELWA campus the day before, with its own unique story.

Dr. Sheik Humarr Khan had been perhaps the most prominent doctor in the fight against Ebola in Sierra Leone. Then Dr. Khan contracted the virus. As part of the research on the drug named ZMapp, one three-dose course was stored in Sierra Leone. When Dr. Khan had become ill, the health officials in Sierra Leone consulted with experts from around the world about whether the ZMapp course should be given to him. The Sierra Leonean officials and the team caring for him decided it was too risky to give an experimental drug to someone as widely esteemed in their country as Dr. Khan. It was undoubtedly a very difficult decision. Dr. Khan died on Tuesday, July 29.

The foam cooler containing the course of ZMapp was transported from Sierra Leone to Foya and flown to Monrovia on Wednesday, where it then was brought to one of the SP offices. One of the three doses was carried, still frozen, to Nancy's house. It was placed under Nancy's armpit to defrost it so that it could be administered to her by IV.

As Lance had talked with experts about ZMapp, he had been advised not to split the doses of ZMapp between Nancy and me. If ZMapp was to work, all three doses would have to be given to the same person.

The decision had been made to give that course to Nancy. I have been credited with sacrificially insisting that the antibodies be given to Nancy instead of me. In truth, the decision was medical, not noble. I had felt a little better early in the day on Wednesday, and progress was being made in setting up an evacuation to the isolation unit at Emory University Hospital in Atlanta, Georgia. Based on descriptions of Nancy's condition, I seemed to be doing better than she at the time of our discussion. I was younger too, and I thought my body could probably handle more than hers.

We did not decide to give the medicine to Nancy because I wanted her to have it; we did so because she needed it more.

John Fankhauser learned Thursday afternoon that I had agreed the antibodies should go to Nancy.

"Up for a quick call?" he texted me.

I called him. Apparently I sounded weaker and was irritated over being alone. I told John that I was dizzy and felt faint when I tried to stand up.

"It sounds like you need a couple of liters of fluid," John told me.

"I don't need fluid, John," I shot back. "I need a doctor."

John said he would get Lance or Linda to come to my house. Then he told me something intriguing: he did not think it would be necessary to give the entire course of antibodies to Nancy. He believed that if Nancy and I could be evacuated as hoped, we could both be started on the antibodies in Monrovia and complete our doses in the United States.

"If you get one dose of the antibodies," he explained, "they are going to get you out of here tomorrow night and you will be in Atlanta in time for your second dose. That will leave two doses here for Nancy, and by the time it's time for her third dose, she will be in Atlanta too. There is no reason not to take it."

"Okay, John," I said. "I am willing to receive one dose if you think Nancy will still be able to get a full course."

∾

Lance checked in on me again in the evening. My breathing was shallow and rapid, and my temperature had risen to 104.

Allison Rolston, a physician's assistant from Tennessee, was a recent arrival to ELWA who had become part of the team taking care of me. With no medical means for cooling me down available, she astutely grabbed some towels, put them in water, and placed the wet towels on top of me. That brought my temperature down a little bit, but I still had a high fever and my rash was worsening.

"I want to give you the antibodies," Lance told me through the window.

"Okay," I said.

Lance was an experienced physician who, after years in palliative care, knew what death looked like—and I was almost there. He told others with him that I was extremely toxic. "Look," Lance told Kendell Kauffeldt, the country director for Samaritan's Purse in Liberia, "you need to get people praying."

Kendell left immediately and began informing everyone on the team, "You need to pray. We are about to lose Kent."

His wife, Bev, was at home when Kendell told her to pray. One son was in bed asleep, and their youngest, eleven-year-old Isaac, was with her. She tried to get him to go to his room, to protect him from whatever news might soon follow.

"No, Mom," he said. "I need to stay here and pray for Uncle Kent."

Bev didn't know how to begin praying. She had no words to say. That is when Isaac prayed aloud: "Dear God, please save Uncle Kent's life, because Ruby and Stephen need their daddy."

THE ZMAPP EXPERIMENT BEGINS

Not knowing if I would live even another hour, Lance made a courageous decision: the ZMapp about to be given to Nancy needed to be given to me.

Two of the doses were still frozen in the cooler. The other was under Nancy's armpit, thawing so she could take it.

Lance went to Nancy's house and told her through a window about his decision. Dr. Debbie had suited up and entered the house. She triple-bagged the vial and decontaminated the package. Lance placed the medicine in a bucket and sped back to my house in a pickup.

I had taken Tylenol around 5 p.m. I was given a fluid bolus between 7 and 8 p.m. along with a dose of Benadryl. The ZMapp was started at just after 8 p.m. I was the first human ever to have ZMapp infused into his body. Nobody knew what to expect.

As the infusion began, I started shaking violently. I was breathing thirty times per minute. That is fast enough to quickly tire out even a normal, healthy person and make him lightheaded.

Breathing that fast and that hard takes up a lot of energy, and the shaking was making it worse. Having been sick as long as I had been and not having eaten more than a few bites for several days, I knew I did not have the energy to sustain that breathing for very long.

I looked over to the nurse practitioner, Tim Mosher, and told him, "I don't know how you are going to breathe for me when I quit breathing, because I can't keep this up."

"Kent," Lance said, "that's the antibodies that are fighting right now. That's what's happening. You've got to let them fight."

Fifteen minutes after the ZMapp had been administered, my temperature was down to 100.0 and my pulse had settled to eighty-four.

Ten minutes after that, the shaking stopped. By 9 p.m., my condition had stabilized. When I sat up in bed, the optimism inside the room and outside the bedroom window soared with the realization that I was going to make it through the night.

Less than a half hour after I was able to sit up in bed, with the ZMapp infusion still running, for the first time in a day and a half, I got up and walked to the bathroom.

During the middle of the night, I walked to the bathroom again. The diarrhea continued, and my temperature increased to 102.5 after midnight, but my breathing was much better.

I was still very sick, but I no longer feared that each breath might be my last.

PART 5

RESCUED!

14

Preparing to Evacuate

Kent

My drastically improved condition made one decision easier: the team leaders had been debating whether to evacuate Nancy or me first, and they determined that Friday probably would be the best time medically to send me back to the United States.

Samaritan's Purse had worked with the US government to request emergency passage out of Liberia for three Americans sick with Ebola virus. In addition to Nancy and me, another nurse with SP had spiked a fever and started vomiting and having diarrhea on Thursday. She turned out to be negative for Ebola, but at the time SP wanted to be prepared in case she did test positive. John Fankhauser remained in quarantine, but he was feeling well and anticipated a negative test that would end his isolation period.

During the on-again, off-again evacuation possibilities that week, I had not cared which country I would go to, whether back to the States or somewhere in Europe. I knew my family could not return to Liberia, so all I wanted was to be taken to a place where my family could come see me. That was important to me. Even if I died, I could at least be close to them instead of on the other side of the world.

I do not know when I learned for certain that I would be flying to Atlanta, but it must have been some time Thursday, because after I received the ZMapp and felt well enough to walk to the bathroom, I started planning out my Friday.

Tim Mosher is a big, strong guy, so I asked him Thursday night if he could come back in the morning and help set me up to take a shower.

Friday morning Tim brought a plastic chair and put it inside the shower. He helped me into the chair and gave me the handheld nozzle. I must have taken a twenty- to thirty-minute shower, and I relished every minute of it. I dried off sitting in the chair because I was too weak to stand up for long, and Tim placed another chair in front of the sink, where I sat and, for the first time in a week, brushed my teeth and put on deodorant.

It was good to experience those milestones with Tim there. He had come to ELWA two or three days earlier, and he had been with me Thursday when I was doing so badly. Once I was feeling better, he told me that he assumed he'd been assigned to take care of me when I was at my sickest and might die, because he was the only one there at the time who didn't know me.

In addition to the ZMapp, another wonderful event had happened Thursday night when Dr. Ed Carns returned! After his brief time with us in April and May when he had been my roommate, Ed had returned home to Oklahoma when it appeared that Liberia had escaped the Ebola outbreak. Then he had come back to work with us in late June/early July when Ebola returned to Liberia, and he'd left just a week before my diagnosis.

When Ed heard I was sick and the hospital badly needed help, he volunteered for another stint.

Ed had flown into Liberia on Thursday night at about the same time I was receiving the ZMapp. He had his driver stop at his house just long enough to drop off his luggage and then came straight to my duplex. He said he had slept five hours on the flight and was ready to step in and help take care of me.

Ed walked into my bedroom carrying two care packages. He opened a Tupperware container to show me a batch of cookies from home.

"Ed, that is really nice," I said. "But the thought of anything sweet makes me want to throw up, so you'd better leave those over there."

The second care package was a plastic grocery bag filled with cards. He handed me a few off the top. The first four were three cards from Stephen and Ruby and one from Amber.

I read the kids' cards followed by Amber's, then told Ed, "I don't have the energy for anymore right now. I just need to rest."

I turned on a slideshow of family pictures on my laptop, thinking for the first time since the diagnosis that I might soon be seeing my family again. Ed sat next to the bed, looking at the pictures and keeping me company until I drifted off. While I slept, Ed remained. He stayed in his PPE well beyond the amount of time we typically wore them, refusing to leave until the arrival of the next person to take care of me. Ed traveled halfway around the world to come sit with me because he had heard I did not like being alone. His presence provided great comfort.

MR. SENTIMENTAL

Ed returned Friday morning, and I was feeling a lot better and stronger. After my shower I asked him to help me pack for my evacuation. Lance had told me I could bring a one-gallon Ziploc bag.

"What about your computer?" Ed asked. "Do you want to take your computer?"

"Oh, I didn't think about that. That's a good idea."

I called Lance and asked if I could also take my laptop in its bag.

"I don't know," he said. "I'll have to ask the pilot."

I hung up and thought for another minute.

"Ed, I can barely walk to the bathroom. I can't carry this bag with my computer in it."

I texted Lance, "Never mind."

I had a black messenger bag that I had received as a Doctor's Day gift during my residency at JPS, and that was the bag I carried to and from the hospital every day.

Ed and I started going through my bag. My stethoscope was too big, so it would stay. The tube of Burt's Bees lip balm made it into the Ziploc bag. My lips were very, very dry. We decided to keep a handful of flash drives that had documents and PowerPoint presentations from conferences. My little black book in which I had written my medical notes was an easy decision to keep.

Ed pulled out my wallet and opened it.

"Your American driver's license?" he asked.

"Ed, I need you to help me," I said. "I am a sentimental person and a little bit of a pack rat. This is not a time for sentimentality—only what is necessary. I need you to help me make those decisions because I can't make them very well on my own right now."

"Okay," he said. "American driver's license. Yes, you need that. Liberian driver's license?"

"I don't need to drive in Liberia."

"Oh. But you want to keep that. It took some effort to get that and you ought to keep it. Starbucks gift card?"

"I have no idea why that is in my wallet. There is no Starbucks in Liberia. I have no idea if there is any credit on it."

"Well, let's keep it."

Then Ed pulled out my credit card.

"I should probably take that," I said.

"No," he countered, "you don't need your credit card. You can get a new one. Throw that away. Debit card?"

"Well, I should probably keep that."

"No," Ed said, "you don't need that. You can get a new one of those. Throw it away. Sam's Club membership card?"

That question made me laugh.

"Look at the picture on the back," I told Ed.

I got the card during college. When I had the photo taken, I had not trimmed my beard in at least two months, and I had just shaved my head as part of a tradition for officers in my social club. I looked like I belonged to some kind of small revolutionary military organization. I had kept the card for laughs.

Ed flipped the card over and chuckled. "This sounds sentimental. You should probably keep this."

"Really?" I questioned. "Not my credit card and debit card, but my Sam's Club card?"

He slid the card into the Ziploc bag.

I decided to keep my American Board of Family Medicine identification card, but not my Liberian medical license card. I didn't think I would be practicing medicine again in Liberia anytime soon.

We also decided that I should back up my computer to an external hard drive and take the hard drive with me.

MAKING PLANS FOR ATLANTA

Amber

After being told Thursday night how much better Kent was doing following his first dose of the medicine, I woke up excited Friday morning.

Friday also was my dad's birthday, and a whole bunch of people came to see us in the guest house: my parents and grandparents, all my brothers and sisters, Kent's parents, his brothers and sisters who live in Texas and their families, my aunt, some cousins. I don't know how many people were there, but it was the most optimistic atmosphere we'd had.

We surprised Dad with a birthday cake and took a group picture holding signs that read "Greetings from Texas" that we would send to Kent.

Around the middle of the day, I received word that Kent would be evacuated—for sure this time—later that day. That set off *another* celebration in our house.

"This is the best birthday ever!" my normally low-key dad exclaimed. "This is the best *day* ever!"

That night was the wedding rehearsal and dinner for my brother Keith and his bride-to-be, Morgan, and Ruby and Stephen had roles in the wedding. After our house cleared out in the afternoon, the three of us lay down for a quick nap. We were so exhausted by all of the tension and excitement that we slept right through the rehearsal and the dinner.

I called my dad. "I'm so sorry. We were asleep."

"It's okay," Dad said. "We will take care of it. The kids will do great."

Kent

I spent the afternoon and evening alternating between backing up my computer and taking naps. Then I received notice that I would need to start getting ready at 9 p.m. and leave for the airport an hour later. We would be on a tight schedule, because for security reasons my ambulance would be allowed on the tarmac only during a designated window of fifteen minutes. Security was really tight for this "black ops" operation.

I was eager to leave and started getting ready ahead of time. I asked Ed for a specific pair of thick, black socks off my shelf and a pair of navy-blue scrubs with my name on them.

When Amber and I had prepared to move to Liberia, I did not own any scrubs. At JPS I had used scrubs from the hospital and had to turn them back in at the end of my residency. I told my mom about my quandary. She had gone into her closet and returned with a stack of navy-blue scrubs. My dad had been a doctor for forty years and never wore scrubs. He preferred to wear a dress shirt and tie to work, which meant that he had scrubs from his hospital that had never been worn. My mom took seven pairs of those scrubs and had "Kent Brantly, MD" embroidered on patches and placed over my dad's name. I wore those scrubs every day in Liberia.

I put on my scrubs and socks and walked into our living room for the first time in a week. Tim Mosher told me to relax on the couch because we would be waiting awhile before I left.

When it came time to leave, Tim had a PPE suit ready for me. He gave me a pair of gloves, a yellow Tychem suit—the thick, heavy-duty one—and heavy, white, rubber boots. He said I did not need to wear goggles or the extra hood. I would have to wear the hood and mask, but I would be able to remove them once I was loaded into the ambulance so I could breathe easier during the trip.

When I say *ambulance,* that requires explanation. Our ambulance was a pickup truck with rails on the sides. The same guys who had converted the kitchen and laundry building into an isolation unit had built a wooden, box-like frame that fit in the bed of the truck, then covered it with blue tarp. That was our ambulance. They also threw in foam cushions and pillows for me to sit on. A second truck had been outfitted the same way, just in case ours encountered problems on the way to the airport.

The best news was that John Fankhauser was fine and had been released from his quarantine. He would be with me in the back of the ambulance. The plan had been for me to ride alone, because we would not be allowed to do any decontaminating on the airport tarmac. Anyone who rode in the back with me would have to ride all the way back to ELWA in full PPE. The airport was forty-five minutes to an hour away—it was a long round trip, but John was willing to embrace it for my sake.

John had tested negative for Ebola shortly before my departure and volunteered to accompany me. He had spent four hours in PPE plenty of times in my house, and he did not want me to be alone.

"At the very least," he said, "we need somebody back there in case Kent has a problem so somebody knows about it. But also, somebody just needs to keep him company."

Amber

Samaritan's Purse let me know that they would send a plane for me the following morning to fly me to Atlanta. And Mary Elizabeth said she would go shopping for me.

"Well, that's really nice of you, but why?" I asked.

"You can't go buy clothes right now," she told me. "It's crazy out there."

"Really?"

"It's crazy out there, and you can't go."

I hadn't been out in public yet, but I knew there were some people in Abilene fearful because the kids and I were there. The three of us were at the center of a controversial international news story, so Mary Elizabeth thought it would be better if I continued to stay out of the public eye.

My sister-in-law, Shelley, flew in from Michigan on Friday to take care of the kids while I went to Atlanta. That meant I would miss my brother Keith's wedding.

Poor Keith and Morgan. Everything happening around me had added enormous stress to their wedding week. Hired professionals backed out of serving at the wedding. Even family members sent their regrets. People were crippled by fear.

Kent

A path had been roped off from my front door to the back of the ambulance/truck, and I think everyone connected with SP was outside of my house, cheering as I shuffled my way to the back of the truck. Carrying a bottle of water, a Gatorade, and my Ziploc bag, I climbed in with John behind me.

Eric Buller, who would be riding in the cab, yelled out, "Amber said she loves you!" She had e-mailed him, asking him to tell me that before my trip. He replied to her, "I told him. Everyone heard it!"

I removed the hood and slipped the mask up to the top of my head. Taking off the mask helped tremendously because although my breathing had improved, it still was not normal. John held my hand as we talked off and on the entire trip.

After they dropped me off at the airport, John rode back to my house in the back of the truck. When he started to get out of the truck to be decontaminated, he noticed that he had been sitting in something wet. His first fear was that I'd had diarrhea, that the fluids had run across the floor of the truck, and that he had been sitting in Ebola for an hour. It turned out that it was spilled bleach water from a bucket that had been placed in the truck in case of an accident.

"Oh, thank the Lord!" John exclaimed.

∾

We arrived at the airport ahead of schedule and had to wait outside a gate for what seemed like a long time. When the gate opened, the truck drove onto the tarmac and stopped beside the plane.

Eric got out of the cab and suited up. I scooted to the end of the truck and was met by Vance Ferebee.

"I am going to be your nurse on the airplane," he said. "We are going to take you home."

Vance, Eric, and John helped me out of the truck, and Vance held my hands and walked backward in front of me to guide me toward the stairs of the jet.

John had not been allowed to get out of the truck, and I turned to face Eric standing nearby on the tarmac. "See ya, man!" was all I said. There was no time for long good-byes or hugs.

15

"Welcome Home"

Kent

I wanted to check out the jet, a specially modified, high-tech Gulfstream III, before boarding. Part of me was thinking, *This is pretty cool! I am getting evacuated out of Liberia in this top-secret jet!* But it took such effort just to put one foot in front of the other that all I really noticed were the plane's flashing lights.

Vance walked up the steps backward, which had to be difficult in his PPE, and helped me climb each step. Then he walked backward down the aisle of the jet and through a plastic, zippered doorway. I passed through that opening, and Vance closed it behind me. There was another entryway ahead of us that Vance unzipped, and then we stepped into the Airborne Biomedical Containment System, which looked like a rectangular transparent tent.

Vance helped me remove my PPE and oriented me to the pod. There was a gurney that reclined, with extra-soft padding. Next to it was a special bucket that would serve as my toilet. The bucket had a lid and contained decontaminating fluids. Vance showed me where the wet wipes and hand sanitizer were, brought me several bottles of water, and asked if I wanted anything to eat. The menu included Oreos and peanut-butter crackers.

"Peanut-butter crackers don't sound bad," I said.

I bit into a cracker, but my mouth was so dry that I had to drink almost a whole bottle of water to get that one cracker down.

Vance assessed that my IV had been in place for several days and decided to place a new line in my left arm. He hooked me up to fluids, handed me a walkie-talkie for communicating with the crew, then asked if I needed anything else.

"Do you have any pull-up-style diapers?" I was wearing the kind with the little, sticky tabs. I could not put those on myself, and I knew I was going to be getting up and going to the bathroom frequently during the flight.

Vance went back out through the first zippered door, yelled out to someone, and came back with a package.

"I'm sorry, this is all we have," he said. He opened the package, and inside were the pull-up diapers I was hoping for.

"Thank God for pull-ups," I told him.

～

We made two fueling stops, at Lajes Air Base in the Azores and at Bangor International Airport in Maine. At Lajes, the pilot was instructed not to open the aircraft door during our stop. At Bangor, not wanting to keep our plane on the ground there longer than necessary, US Customs cleared us in record time. At both stops a crew member came into the pod to check on me. I was alone the rest of the time.

I was so dehydrated that I had an insatiable thirst the whole trip. It seemed like every time I dozed off, I woke up five minutes later needing a drink.

To go to the bathroom, I had to stand up and spin around to sit on the bucket. Just that little bit of activity required so much energy and took so long that by the time I was ready to wipe or get up, I had to decide whether I wanted to go through the whole process of cleaning my hands with sanitizer and spinning back to the bed before I could take another drink. I was not sure if I could go that long without water. I was so thirsty that a lot of times, I grabbed my bottle and took a drink before getting off the bucket.

At the Lajes stop, the crew doctor, Doug Olson, put a couple of leads on my chest so they could watch my heart rhythm on a monitor. I also had a pulse oximeter on my finger to monitor the oxygen saturation of my blood. The cord was not long enough to reach the bucket, and every time I got up and spun around, I had to remove the pulse ox.

During the check-in at the Bangor airport, I was asked how many times I had used the bucket and how many times I had diarrhea.

I wasn't counting, but it was a lot. I pretty much operated on a cycle of returning to bed from the bucket, taking a drink, dozing off, waking up after a few minutes to take another drink, and spinning to the bucket again. I told them I had no idea and suggested they look at the monitor, because every time I took off the pulse ox, I was going to the bucket.

The crew told me during the flight that the humidity inside the airplane was 14 percent. I thought, *Are you trying to kill me?* I had been living in the high humidity of Liberia and then suddenly had been placed into the other end of the humidity spectrum. I was certain this drastic change would not be helpful, given my severe dehydration from constant diarrhea.

Over the course of the fourteen-hour trip, I drank seven or eight half-liter bottles of water.

∞

Our plane landed at Dobbins Air Reserve Base outside Atlanta at just after 11 a.m. Eastern time. The third medical crew member I had not met yet, nurse Jonathan Jackson, came into the pod and helped me into a new suit. The crew had placed pads on the floor of the plane and drapes over the seats. Because I had geared up inside the pod, my suit had to be treated as contaminated along with anything my suit touched.

One of the two paramedics from the waiting ambulance, John Arevalo, came into the plane and greeted me. John assisted me down the aisle and through the zippered entryway. He led, walking backward as Vance had done when I entered the plane. On the steps descending from the plane, someone had to call out each step for John because he could not see them because of his PPE.

We took our time going down the steps. When we reached flat ground, I was definitely weak and exhausted, but I had made the descent without any trouble.

A stretcher was waiting for me, and once I was secured on the stretcher, John looked down at me and said, "Welcome home."

The inside of the ambulance—a real ambulance, not a pickup with wooden rails—had been modified so that if anything spilled, the fluids would be contained. A second ambulance had been prepared in the same manner in case something happened to our ambulance on the way to the hospital. They did not tell me this then, but they had taken into account the possibility that someone opposed to my being brought into the United States might try to disrupt the ambulance trip.

It's funny that at ELWA and in Atlanta, both teams that transported me had the same idea of preparing a backup ambulance, but for very different reasons. In Atlanta they anticipated the possibility of sabotage. At ELWA my SP friends feared our truck would break down.

The drive from Dobbins to Emory was about thirty minutes. I had no clue that news helicopters were overhead and our motorcade was being televised live all across the nation. I've heard my ambulance trip compared to O. J. Simpson's infamous ride in the white Ford Bronco.

Many people have told me that they remember where they were when they watched the first patient with Ebola touch American soil, wondering what would happen next.

AN INSPIRING WALK

John, the paramedic, had walked with me off the plane, and when the ambulance came to a stop in a utility parking lot at Emory, he asked, "Do you think you can walk into the hospital?"

"How far is it?" I asked.

"Not far at all—it's just right there," he said. "But when we get inside, there are some more stairs."

"How many steps is it?" I asked. "Is it more or less than the jet?"

Exiting the jet had been difficult and exhausting, and I wasn't sure if I could walk up more steps than the airplane had.

"It is probably more, but they are not as big and they are not as steep," he said. "If you can't do it, we will take you in on the stretcher. Not a problem. But if you can do it, there is an entrance right here that will take us to where we need to go."

"Okay," I said.

Again, I had no idea that helicopter cameras were trained on our ambulance, waiting for the back door to open. John backed out of the ambulance and onto the ground, then extended his right hand to hold mine. The door to my left was open, and I grabbed on to it with my left hand to steady myself, and then put my left foot down on the step, followed by my right foot. The next step down to the ground was farther, but I made it fine, again left foot first.

John stepped around to my left to close the ambulance door, held both of my hands, and walked on my left side toward a back entrance of the hospital. The cameras recorded me walking gingerly. When we had landed at Dobbins and the nurse had come into the pod to help me suit up, I asked if I needed to put on my rubber boots, because they were heavy.

"Do you need to keep them for some reason?" he asked.

"No."

He figured it would be easier for me to walk without having to carry the boots, then he assured me he would destroy them.

When we arrived at the hospital, I was only wearing my booties and the path from the ambulance was gravel. My steps were measured because I was practically walking barefoot on gravel.

I have watched video of my arrival, and commentators speculated about what might be inside the bag I was carrying with both hands. That wasn't medicine, as some wondered aloud, or anything medical even. That was my one-gallon Ziploc bag of personal items, including—yes—my old Sam's Club membership card.

Out of sight of the news cameras, we reached the stairs just inside the hospital door. John sensed that I was getting tired and asked if I wanted to take a break. I nodded. John gave me a quick breather, then we went up the steps and into the hallway just outside the isolation unit.

My walking from the ambulance to the hospital is probably the one thing people bring up the most when we talk. Most medical-expert commentators were surprised. Some called my walking in "a miracle." Some remarked that it was an encouraging sign for my chances of recovery.

Franklin Graham had asked the Samaritan's Purse vice presidents during a meeting four days earlier, "Wouldn't it be a testimony to the power of Jesus Christ if Kent Brantly walked off that airplane?"

Watching someone you love or are concerned about strapped to a stretcher and being wheeled into a hospital by paramedics can be defeating. It is never encouraging. Although I was not trying to make a statement by choosing to walk in, my thirty-second walk really resonated with people who witnessed it.

So many people had been praying for me, and I think to see me walking when they anticipated that I was on death's doorstep served as a live picture of answered prayer. I have been told countless times, "When we saw you walk out of that ambulance, we just praised God."

"THAT'S HIM!"

Amber

I was antsy Saturday morning before flying out to Atlanta with Kent's parents, his sister Krista, Mary Elizabeth, and Melissa. The plane from Samaritan's Purse arrived, and the pilot, Keith Anderson, invited me to fly in the copilot's seat. We talked the entire flight, and his words were such an encouragement.

When we landed in Atlanta, Tim Viertel and his posse met us. Tim was SP's vice president of security and a retired Secret Service agent. Imagine an intimidating, six-foot-seven person with a teddy bear's heart—that's Tim. He became my bodyguard, personal assistant, chauffeur, and general gorilla. I hadn't considered before that I might need security, but Kent's arrival in the United States was generating controversy, because some people adamantly believed it was a big mistake to allow anyone with Ebola into our country.

Tim and his group of former Secret Service guards put us in two black Suburbans with darkly tinted windows and drove us to a hotel. They didn't want the name Brantly to show up anywhere, so they checked us in under pseudonyms. I became Becky Woodall.

I wanted to go directly to the hospital, but we couldn't because security was very tight and the media presence was crazy over Kent's impending arrival. Tim said hospital security had told him there was an alternate route we could take to the hospital but that they needed us to go to our hotel and wait there until Kent had settled in.

Tim said it could be a while before we could go to the hospital and suggested we order room service. Kent's mom used her real name for her order, and when she realized what she had done, she got nervous that she had ruined our cover.

I was in a room with Krista, Mary Elizabeth, and Melissa, and we turned on the television. I, like seemingly everyone else in America, watched Kent's ambulance driving down the freeway. We picked up the pace of our eating as we watched.

When the ambulance came to a stop at the hospital, our sense of expectation peaked. I didn't know what I would see next.

The two men in PPEs stepped out of the ambulance, and the commentators began speculating who they were.

"Do you think that is the doctor?"

"Do you think that is really him?"

"Surely they sent a decoy. I'm sure he is coming in a different way."

When the person on the right took his first steps, I shouted, "That's him! I know that's Kent! He's here!"

"That *is* Kent!" Krista said, then she sat on the bed and started bawling.

I don't think I even took time to process what it meant that Kent was walking instead of on a stretcher. I had already seen all of the news coverage I needed to see.

I called Tim. "Let's go! He's here—let's go!"

Tim and his crew met us in the hallway and escorted us out the back door of the hotel for the ride to the hospital in the Suburbans.

When we arrived at Emory, Tim and a hospital policeman named Tyrone led us through tunnels to Kent's unit instead of taking us through a public entrance. Hospitals have tunnels that most people don't get to see, and it was kind of exciting making our way through Emory's. Not that I was interested in sightseeing, though.

I was walking really fast at the front of our group because I was so ready to get to Kent.

We made it to the Serious Communicable Diseases Unit (SCDU) and had to wait until we were told we could go back to see him. But just knowing Kent was right around the corner made a huge difference for me. Several hospital administrators came to welcome us and make us feel at home. They seemed pleased and excited to have Kent there.

We met Dr. Bruce Ribner, a nice, gentle man who was the director of the SCDU. Sharon Vanairsdale, the unit's clinical nurse specialist, came in to introduce herself and gave me the phone number to Kent's room.

Of course, I had to call it right away. Dr. Aneesh Mehta, Kent's admitting physician, was in the room and answered the phone.

"This is Aneesh."

"Is Dr. Brantly available?"

"Yes, he is. He's right here." His voice was so calm, cordial, and reassuring.

In a moment Kent was on the phone, and it was such a relief to hear his voice.

"I'm glad you are here," he told me.

"I am too," I said. "Whenever they are ready to let me back there to see you, I am here waiting. I love you!"

It wasn't long before a nurse came to take me back to see Kent. The SCDU had two patient rooms on opposite sides of an anteroom, which was like a nurse's station between the rooms. There was a window on the door to Kent's room, and to the left of the door was a small desk with a telephone-intercom. A smaller window was above the intercom. That window faced directly toward Kent's bed, with the head of the bed at the far wall.

Kent was lying down, and he looked exhausted. He was puffy with swelling and his eyes were bloodshot red.

Anyone else looking at Kent would have said he looked pretty bad. But he looked good to me. It was so wonderful to see him.

"How was your trip?" I asked him through the intercom.

"It was a trip," he answered.

"We watched you walk off that ambulance."

"You were watching me?"

"Oh, Kent, the whole world was watching you."

I would have liked to talk with Kent longer, but Dr. Mehta and Jill Morgan, the nurse, were still making their initial assessments, checking his IV, drawing blood, those kinds of things. As a nurse, I knew they could do their jobs better with Kent's full attention.

Kent

Dr. Mehta had told me that only Amber would be allowed to see me until I had some time to rest. When he saw how much talking with Amber lifted my spirits, he and Jill decided to let my other family members come into the anteroom one at a time.

I had not cried on any of my phone calls with my family when I was in Monrovia. But when my mom, then my dad, and then Krista came back, I cried as I talked with each one.

Amber

Relief and hope were my dominant feelings after seeing Kent. I could tell he had improved since seeing him in our FaceTime chats, but he still had taken only one dose of the ZMapp with two more to go, and we couldn't know how his body would react to the experimental treatment.

I wasn't naive. I knew it was still uncertain whether he would survive.

16

Reunited with Nancy

Kent

Although I never again felt that impending sense of doom like I had the Thursday when I could barely breathe, I still was very, very sick early in my stay in the SCDU at Emory.

Within my first twenty-four hours there, I went through twenty-eight bedpans. That is not the number of times I had diarrhea; the total was higher than that. I would get out of bed to use the bedside commode and sit there for about ten minutes while I had diarrhea. Then I would get up and start to spin back into bed and have to hurry back to the toilet with more diarrhea before the bedpan could be changed.

The first day my fever was 102.0, and my heart rate was 120 beats per minute.

I had hepatitis too, because the virus had affected my liver. My liver condition also was made worse by the amount of Tylenol I had taken in Liberia. A few years ago the recommended daily maximum for Tylenol was reduced from four grams per day to three. I had been taking four grams a day since I had first developed a fever—taking two extra-strength Tylenol every six hours around the clock.

Because of the meals I had skipped while working at ELWA, my weight had dropped from 198 to 165 pounds since I'd arrived in Liberia. When they weighed me in bed at Emory, I expected to hear an even lower number because I had barely eaten in days and had experienced copious diarrhea. To my surprise I weighed 178 pounds.

"That is impossible," I told the nurse.

"Kent, you are swollen," she told me.

I looked down to my legs and for the first time noticed how swollen they were. My whole body was so puffy that I could push a finger into my skin and leave an indentation.

I knew I was still sick. I still had Ebola. I knew all too well that my body still was fighting a disease that had a 70 percent chance of killing me.

Amber

Kent's doctors were careful not to give us any false hope. They would remind me, "He's not out of the woods yet. We are cautiously optimistic." Dr. Ribner used that phrase "cautiously optimistic" a lot.

My parents and sister, Caryn, flew into Atlanta on Sunday after the wedding and celebration, and they were able to see Kent from the anteroom. That was the day Kent received his second dose of ZMapp.

Kent

One of the biggest medical advantages of being in Atlanta compared to Monrovia was the laboratory capabilities. Emory's staff could perform chemistries that we could not at ELWA, where it was not safe to take an Ebola patient's blood into the hospital lab.

John Fankhauser had assumed that my potassium was low because of the amount of diarrhea I was having, so he'd given me potassium in my fluids. But he had no way to check my potassium levels to see if he was giving me the right amount. Potassium is an electrolyte that is especially tenuous, because it must remain within a specific range. If your potassium gets too low, you can develop a fatal abnormal heart rhythm. And the same is true if it gets too high.

When potassium is given to a patient, kidney function must be monitored.

The kidneys help maintain the proper concentration of potassium in the blood, so if they are not working well, the potassium level can increase rapidly.

Since the doctors at ELWA could not run any blood tests on Ebola patients, they just had to watch how much I was urinating to see if my kidneys were still working. John and the other doctors had to use their medical knowledge and clinical judgment to treat me without the aid of important medical technology that we take for granted in the Western medical world. Later during my recovery I had the opportunity to review all my lab results side by side with the existing research on Ebola. During my worst times, I had felt physically that I was dying, but it was sobering reading in medical terms how close I really had come to death.

Certain laboratory values indicate an increased risk of dying. When I read my results, I had at least three of those laboratory markers after arriving at Emory: dangerously low sodium, potassium, and albumin levels.

Reading the lab numbers also provided data to support what I believed: John and my colleagues at ELWA had saved my life. They did an amazing, incredible job despite practicing medicine in a resource-limited setting and battling a vicious disease.

Amber

The next morning, Monday, I received a phone call from Lance Plyler in Monrovia telling me that Nancy had received her second dose of ZMapp and showed signs of improvement. I couldn't wait to tell Kent, so I wrote him a note and asked a nurse to give it to him.

This was Kent's second full day at Emory, and his condition seemed to take a step forward. The lab report showed that his electrolyte level was improving. His diarrhea began easing too, with formed material visible for the first time. That day Kent told the nurses that he wanted to get up and walk around the room. The nurses said Kent was in good spirits and staying positive, and suggested he needed books and crossword puzzles to occupy his time.

"He's doing great," Dr. Mehta told me, "but he's not out of the woods yet."

Kent was weak when he stood and still needed assistance to his bedside commode, but the fact that he wanted to walk around was a very uplifting sign.

Kent

Tuesday was my mom's birthday, but the big news was Nancy's arrival at Emory. I had been so worried when I was told that her plane had left Liberia. That flight had been extremely difficult for me, and my condition had improved immediately prior to my trip. Nancy, from what I had gathered, was in worse shape than I had been boarding the plane, and she was twenty-six years older.

With Nancy about to arrive in the SCDU, the need for security and space meant that Amber and other family members needed to clear out. Amber and I talked on the phone as I watched television coverage of Nancy's flight landing late that morning at Dobbins, then her escorted ride to the hospital in the same ambulance I had arrived in.

The ambulance stopped at the hospital, and they unloaded Nancy on a stretcher.

"I have to hang up," I told Amber. "They are going to bring her in here. I want to see her."

The other patient room in the unit was about twenty feet from mine, and I waved to Nancy as she was wheeled in. She was all bundled up in her suit and strapped to the stretcher. Her head was reclined, and all I could see of her was her face. Either she could not see me waving because of her PPE, or she was not responsive enough to acknowledge me.

I was so glad that she had made it to Atlanta and that we were in the same place together, but I was scared for her.

CHICK-FIL-A!

I ate my first meal that evening—chicken broth and Jell-O. It was the best chicken broth I've ever tasted, and I ate every single bit of it. I drank a lot of fluids under doctor's orders, including Boost protein shakes. Amber was able that day to get me Gatorade, gum, and more much-needed lip balm.

I still had a slight fever, at 100.8, and my chest hurt when I inhaled. But I believed that to be musculoskeletal and not heart related.

The doctors were pleased with my ability to drink a lot of fluids, and the nurses noted that my eyes were nearly clear compared to being so red when I arrived. I also received an encouraging report from the doctors: my viral load had not increased between the second and third doses of ZMapp. Based on that, the doctors expected that the third dose would cause the viral load to go down and that it would stay down.

I received my third and final dose of ZMapp on Wednesday afternoon. I did not know what to expect from that point, and I don't think the doctors did either. I was the first human to take the medicine; this was uncharted territory. How could the doctors know what to do next?

I felt adventurous that evening and told Amber that I wanted food from a place our family loved and had not eaten at in almost a year: Chick-fil-A.

Amber brought me a number one combo: a chicken sandwich, waffle fries, and a large sweet tea without ice. She also got me a strawberry shake.

I had eaten about two-thirds of the sandwich and some of the fries when I looked at the nurse and said, "I have to go to the bathroom right now."

I pushed my tray aside, and she helped me get up. Before I could even turn around, the diarrhea hit. I made a huge mess. I think that might have been that nurse's first shift with me too. Another nurse came in to help, and they got me cleaned up and back into bed. Then they had to clean the room.

That was our first "spill" in the unit, and Sean Kaufman, the safety and compliance officer, came and stood at the door with his protocol manual and talked the nurses through each and every step. They cleaned up the mess and decontaminated everything as though they had done it dozens of times.

That was a surreal moment when I realized, *Wow! These nurses are taking care of the first Ebola patient in America. No one has ever done what they are doing. They have to clean this deadly toxic mess in a safe way, and these nurses have volunteered to work in this unit—to care for me.*

Amber

Dr. Ribner got on to me a little about the Chick-fil-A. "You as a nurse ought to know better than to feed him fried food on his first meal," he told me.

"That is all he wanted," I said defensively.

Kent

I had been having trouble sleeping, having really active dreams. In one dream I was in a competition: I needed to accomplish something for my team, and I could not get it done. I would wake up with my sheets wet from sweat. I considered the sweat a product of sleeping on a vinyl mattress, not fever. The nurses said they would give me diazepam and morphine at 7 p.m. and again at 3 a.m.

Anticipating a good night's sleep, I texted Amber near the end of Wednesday, "Feeling good. Going to sleep soon with a little medical help. It has been a great day. I love you. Praise God for his mercy. Good night. Love you."

WORTH CELEBRATING

Thursday was a momentous day in my room: I showered! One of the nurses wrote in my chart: "First shower. He is very happy."

After my shower—a nice, long, soaking, thirty minutes—I put on a pair of sweatpants, a T-shirt, and new underwear Amber had brought me. I texted her, "Guess who is wearing sweatpants like a real person?" Following every shower, I had to put on new clothes because my old clothes were contaminated and had to be destroyed.

I was hungry again on Thursday despite the Chick-fil-A episode. This time I opted for nonfried hospital food. For me, the return of my appetite was the first solid sign that I was going to recover. I could eat, and my diarrhea was slowing.

This was one of those embarrassing routines: every time I used the restroom, the nurse had to look inside the toilet and describe what I had produced. As I progressively felt better, I did not have a nurse inside the unit with me twenty-four hours a day, and when I used the bathroom while alone, I had to note how much there was and what it looked like and give a report to the nurse in the anteroom.

Thursday was the first time I was able to walk to the bathroom—not the bedside toilet—with assistance. And then my diarrhea wasn't all watery. I high-fived the nurse in my room. A high-five over diarrhea may sound odd, but that was a moment worthy of celebration.

∽

On Friday, August 8, I did not have a fever for the first time in sixteen days. Regularly going to the bathroom on my own now, I asked the nurses if I could have my blood-pressure cuff removed. I was hooked up to continuous monitors and had to unhook each time I needed to go to the bathroom. I also felt strong enough to talk with the most visitors I had entertained to that point. During the day, at the suggestion of Samaritan's Purse, I wrote my first press release:

> I am writing this update from my isolation room at Emory University
> Hospital, where the doctors and nurses are providing the very best care
> possible. I am growing stronger every day, and I thank God for his mercy
> as I have wrestled with this terrible disease. I also want to extend my deep
> and sincere thanks to all of you who have been praying for my recovery, as
> well as for Nancy and for the people of Liberia and West Africa.
>
> My wife Amber and I, along with our two children, did not move
> to Liberia for the specific purpose of fighting Ebola. We went to Liberia
> because we believe God called us to serve him at ELWA Hospital.
>
> One thing I have learned is that following God often leads us to
> unexpected places. When Ebola spread into Liberia, my usual hospital

work turned more and more toward treating the increasing number of Ebola patients. I held the hands of countless individuals as this terrible disease took their lives away from them. I witnessed the horror firsthand, and I can still remember every face and name.

When I started feeling ill on that Wednesday morning, I immediately isolated myself until the test confirmed my diagnosis three days later. When the result was positive, I remember a deep sense of peace that was beyond all understanding. God was reminding me of what he had taught me years ago, that he will give me everything I need to be faithful to him.

Now it is two weeks later, and I am in a totally different setting. My focus, however, remains the same—to follow God. As you continue to pray for Nancy and me, yes, please pray for our recovery. More importantly, pray that we would be faithful to God's call on our lives in these new circumstances.

HOOPS IN ISOLATION

Beginning that weekend, my condition started improving more rapidly. My labs were moving closer to the normal values, and Dr. G. Marshall Lyon III told Amber that his only concern was that I could "go stir-crazy" inside the unit.

I never felt like I was going stir-crazy. I was tired of being in the unit, and I was ready to get out of the hospital. But I was thankful to be alive, and if I would have had to stay in that unit for another month, I honestly would have been okay with that.

Both Saturday and Sunday I placed phone calls to people who were important to me, such as close friends, ministers, and mentors. As my recovery gained speed, I was feeling a sense of appreciation for being alive, and I wanted to reach out to those people to thank them for how they had impacted me and for their prayers.

On Tuesday, August 12, doctors from Emory and the CDC collaborated to determine a medical threshold for when Nancy and I could be released. It was important that our releases be handled in a way that would not cause panic and fear in the general public.

Emory and the CDC decided that we could leave the hospital after two consecutive negative Ebola tests, taken at least twenty-four hours apart. My most recent blood test had been positive, so I would have to wait to be retested.

One of the nurses, Crystal Johnson, came in one morning, sat rubber therapy bands on my bedside table, and announced, "You're going to start exercising today."

I worked with the therapy bands every day, and even began doing push-ups and squats. The first day of exercises, I did one push-up. After a week, I was up to fifteen per day. That's not many, but it was not easy after what my body had been through. Some of the nurses did push-ups alongside me to encourage me.

After I had been exercising and building up my strength, Jill Morgan set up a NERF basketball goal over the top of a door in my room, which the nurses had designated "Kent's Man Cave" with a handwritten sign in my window.

Every shift, some of the nurses came in and played H-O-R-S-E with me. We created crazy shots, reminiscent of "The Showdown," the famous McDonald's Larry Bird–Michael Jordan commercial: "From the corner, behind the bed, off the wall . . . nothing but net."

I lost only one time . . . to Haley Durr. Her win made big news in the unit.

"I do have Ebola," I reminded the nurses. "So let's not get too excited about beating the guy with Ebola."

The nurses tried to claim that they were at a disadvantage because they had to play in PPE.

That was just an excuse as far as I was concerned. I would have gladly traded playing with Ebola for playing in a full suit.

By the end of the week, based only on how I felt, I was ready to leave. Now when he gave Amber an update on my condition, Dr. Lyon was using the word "fantastic." My platelet count had been low at first, then had rebounded to higher than normal. That was now coming down, my kidney labs were good, my liver was improving, and although my albumin level remained low, it was increasing.

෨

The weekend of August 16–17, all five of my siblings and my parents gathered in Atlanta to see me.

I shed tears as I talked with each of them, recounting various parts of my story. When I had talked with them on the phone from Liberia, when they learned I had tested positive, they were crying, but I wasn't. Seeing them in Atlanta, though, it was like I was finally allowed to cry.

Up to that point I had focused all my mental and emotional energies on beating Ebola—even on taking my next breath that Thursday night. But now I felt like I was coming off a lengthy adrenaline rush and could finally begin to process my experience.

My brothers and sisters also would go out in groups to the utility parking lot and call me from a cell phone. My second-story window overlooked that lot, and I could walk to the window to wave to them and talk while seeing them.

That turned out to be a big weekend for my parents. Since there are six kids in my family, it is not often that we are all together. But we were at the hospital, even though there was that one little matter of my being isolated in my room.

෨

By this point I had developed a ravenous appetite. There was a menu in my room for ordering from the cafeteria. I would tell the nurse in my room what I wanted, and he would write down my order on a dry-erase board, then hold it up against the door window for a nurse in the anteroom to read.

One morning I looked at the printout of my order that came with my tray, and the cafeteria workers had written "Have a great day" with a smiley face to me.

A routine breakfast for me was two orders of scrambled eggs, two orders of pancakes, two orders of bacon, fruit salad, Greek yogurt, a box of granola, orange juice, coffee, and my chocolate Boost.

The nurses liked to tease me about how much I was ordering. "Anything else?" they would ask.

I would eat all my breakfast and then ask Amber for another cup of coffee.

Throughout the day, I would ask family members for more food. One time that weekend, my brothers Chad and Kevin said they were going to pick up burgers and asked if I wanted them to bring me anything. Of course. I was always hungry.

"One or two burgers?" they asked.

"Depends on how big they are," I said. "Go ahead and get two."

They brought two half-pound bacon cheeseburgers that came in separate foam containers, one with onion rings and one with french fries. I ate all of one burger and half of the second, all the onion rings, and most of the fries.

AN UNEXPECTED TREAT

At some point during this time, after I was clearly feeling fine and walking around, Amber was in the anteroom talking to me over the phone. Sean, the safety compliance officer, was also in the anteroom—we were always "chaperoned" when we talked—and he cracked open my door and said, "Come over here."

I looked at him funny, and he said, "Come stand over here."

I put the phone down and walked over. He made me put a glove on. Amber always wore gloves in the anteroom. When I put my glove on, he held the door so that Amber and I could hold hands. That was an incredible feeling. That was the first contact we'd had with each other since she and the kids had left Liberia almost a month earlier.

Amber

I didn't know what Sean had planned when he called Kent to the door. I had wanted to hug Kent and hold his hand since the first time I saw him in the unit, but I also didn't want to touch him until it was completely safe.

Even though we were wearing gloves, I could still feel his fingers and the bones in his hand. I don't think I'll ever forget how special that moment was. My rush of emotions surprised me.

In some ways my feelings were comparable to that time years earlier in my car when Kent had held my hand and told me that he liked me—and the idea of my being in his future.

17

Ebola Free!

Kent

As I began to feel better and had more time to think and process my experience, I began trying to figure out how I had contracted Ebola. I had been certain that our process, our protocols, and our equipment in the treatment unit were safe. We always worked as a team to keep each other safe as we cared for patients. There had been no obvious breach of protocol.

While working in the treatment unit, I had continued to take call for obstetrics and was constantly evaluating patients in the triage tent or ER who had symptoms suspicious for Ebola. I was convinced that my contact must have come from one of these patients.

While I will never know for sure, I concluded that the most likely time was the night of July 14, nine days before my illness began.

I was at home—it was the first night we had an all-Liberian crew in the ETU, led by a physician's assistant from the Ministry of Health. I was on call as backup in case they needed any help. I decided to run up to the hospital around 8 p.m. to make sure everything was under control. As I expected, everything in the unit was running per protocol.

As I prepared to head home, Dr. Biligan Korha, the general practitioner on call for the hospital, asked me to evaluate a thirty-year-old obstetrical patient she was concerned about. The patient had arrived a short time earlier in serious condition. At thirty-two weeks pregnant, she developed a dangerous condition known as eclampsia, which is high blood pressure and seizures in pregnancy. When her husband had brought her to the ER, the woman was still convulsing. As her seizures subsided, initial lab tests revealed severe malaria, and a quick ultrasound by Dr. Korha showed the baby was no longer living.

Dr. Korha wanted me to evaluate the woman, because she had a fever and had begun having black, runny diarrhea after arrival in the labor ward. She wondered if the patient might have Ebola. The only thing to do was to carefully move her to the Ebola treatment unit and offer supportive care until we confirmed her Ebola status.

After doing our best for that patient and decontaminating the labor ward, ER, and sidewalk—everywhere the patient had been—I headed toward my car. But Dr. Korha chased me down. Another older woman was in the ER with symptoms suspicious for Ebola. That patient had run a fever and had suffered with diarrhea for three or four days, her eyes were red, and her husband had died one week earlier of an unknown cause.

As I carefully gathered her history from her daughter, the patient motioned for help and the daughter helped her get out of bed and go to the bathroom—a routine that had been repeated several times since she had come to the ER. The daughter was very distrustful of the health-care system and of me as a foreigner, but she did eventually allow her mother to be transferred to the isolation unit. The daughter never returned to our hospital after that night, and that was the last time I saw her.

Both patients died the next morning. Postmortem tests showed that the pregnant woman had not died from Ebola, but from the complications of her pregnancy. The older woman, though, did have Ebola.

At Emory, as I reflected on the details of that night, I remembered that as I had counseled the daughter and tried to persuade her that taking her mother into the isolation unit was best for her, I was sure I had held the daughter's hands. I might have put my arm around her shoulders too. Because we had not seen her again, there had been no way to ask if she had been sick and not told us, or whether she had washed her hands after helping her mother in the bathroom.

I wondered too whether I had touched my face after my contact with the daughter.

I will never know the answers to those questions.

WAVING GOOD-BYE TO NANCY

I had blood tests again Friday and Saturday. On Monday, August 18, Dr. Jay Varkey suited up and came into the room with my test results. Amber joined the conversation on the intercom. Ebola still was present in my blood.

"But your tests are getting less and less positive," he said.

I told Dr. Varkey that I wanted to talk to him about Nancy.

She and I had talked by phone every day since she had arrived. Initially, we had short conversations because we both were weak. As time went on, we talked more and more, as often as three times a day, sometimes as long as an hour each time.

Together, we processed what we were going through: "How are you feeling? Are you able to eat? How is your appetite? Did you have this experience like me?"

We also processed what we had been through in Liberia, caring for patients together in the ELWA unit and then both getting sick there. We contemplated what life would be like when we left Emory.

A bond developed between us that we will share for the rest of our lives, and it is a bond that could not have been formed with any other person in the world. It is exclusively ours, because we are the only two people who went through exactly what the other experienced.

Through our conversations, it seemed obvious to me that I was doing better than Nancy. I was starting to regain my strength and doing exercises in my room. Nancy, however, still seemed very weak.

I would tell Nancy to drink her protein shakes and exercise. "Get out of bed and do your exercises," I'd urge her. "I am doing squats over here. Come on, you need to do squats with me."

Nancy told me she knew I was feeling better when I started treating her as though I were her doctor.

She had been experiencing problems that I was not. Her sodium level required more time to come under control than mine, and she was also having nerve pain in her feet.

Everything indicated that I was further along the path of recovery than Nancy.

"I am concerned about her," I told Dr. Varkey. "I don't know how Nancy is going to do if I get out of here before her, because we are talking every day, and I physically feel like I am doing so much better than she is. I am exercising every day, doing push-ups and squats, and she is not up to that level of activity yet."

"What if Nancy left the hospital before you?" Amber asked.

"That is a reality you might want to consider," Dr. Varkey said. Then he went over to Nancy's room and informed her that her test results were negative and that she would be getting out of isolation that night.

When Nancy left the isolation unit for a regular hospital room, I watched from the window in my door. She walked over toward me, and they let us put on gloves and hold each other's hand for a minute.

I was so happy for her, but at the same time I was sad. Although we had talked daily, we had not been able to see much of each other. Even when we both had the strength to stand at our windows, it was hard to get a good look at her across the anteroom and through both windows.

Holding Nancy's hand at my door, I could see the toll that Ebola had taken on her body. She had lost so much weight, and it looked like she had taken a beating. Taking on Ebola is a fight—a fight for your life.

Even in Nancy's physical weakness, though, the strength of her faith showed true.

"To God be the glory," she kept saying as we talked.

Her vibrant personality and concern for others also shone through. She was kind of upset that we were not getting out at the same time. I think she was a little worried that I would be devastated that she was getting out before me.

I wasn't though; I was relieved.

I had worried in Liberia that I would lose my friend while also facing the possibility that I might die. In part because I was afraid to call Nancy, we had talked probably only twice while we were both sick in Liberia. In some ways I felt responsible for Nancy getting Ebola, because I was the boss when we were in the unit and assumed responsibility for all the members of my team. As I had laid in my bed and thought about Ebola's 70 percent mortality rate—and higher where we were—simple math told me that with the two of us sick, odds were that at least one of us would not make it.

But as we released hands and Nancy turned to leave the isolation unit to reunite with her husband, I felt no anxiety. My friend was okay. I was alive, and Nancy had made it too.

Amber

Kent called me at the hotel late that night and told me that Nancy had been moved out of isolation in preparation for being discharged.

I got nervous at the thought of her leaving without me getting to see her, so I woke up very early Tuesday morning and raced to the hospital.

"Is she still here? Has she left?" I asked the nurses.

They informed me that she was in her new room.

I had made it to the hospital so early that I beat Nancy's husband to her room!

She was already dressed and ready to go when I walked in. We were able to sit together for an hour and talk, holding hands the entire time. Then David, her husband, came into the room and they finished up all her paperwork for the discharge.

The hospital had not announced that Nancy would be leaving—her departure would be much quieter than her arrival. Nancy and David had friends who came to pick them up where Kent had unloaded from his ambulance. After her friends arrived in her room, I walked out with them.

On our way down the hallway, we walked past the isolation unit. The nurses held the door into the anteroom open and Kent's door open. Kent and Nancy waved to each other, and Kent took pictures with his phone.

Nancy hugged her doctors and nurses on her way out, at least the ones who were there. The rest would not know until they reported to work that Nancy had been discharged. She left the hospital quietly, exactly the way she wanted.

OUT OF ISOLATION

Kent

Amber and I had talked with the doctors about how we would coordinate my release, and we worked out the details of a press conference once my blood test was negative.

They had taken my blood on Sunday and Tuesday. On Wednesday, August 20, I was told I had the two successive negative blood tests I needed. I was Ebola free!

Then everything happened in a whirlwind.

The first order of business was to get me out of the isolation unit. As with everything else in the unit, there were detailed steps that had to be followed.

I gave them my wedding ring to have it decontaminated and took a good shower. One of the nurses gave me a sample-sized bottle of Versace shower gel.

"When you come out to meet your woman for the first time," he told me, "you need to smell good."

I used the entire bottle.

When I finished my shower, a nurse handed me a clean towel to dry off with. Then I put on clean hospital scrubs. I walked across clean towels that had been placed on the floor, stopped at the doorway, put on clean hospital socks, and cleaned my hands with hand sanitizer. I walked through the door and into the anteroom, where I again cleaned my hands with sanitizer. Amber was waiting for me in the hallway, and when I stepped out of the anteroom, she gave me a big hug.

Then we kissed and I was thinking, *Are we allowed to do this?* The look on Amber's face told me Amber was wondering the same thing!

Jill, who had been my first nurse at Emory, had stayed after her shift to witness my leaving the unit. She had given my decontaminated wedding ring to Amber, and Amber slid the band back onto my ring finger.

From there I was taken to a regular hospital room for the night. It was the same room that Nancy had stayed in.

Amber left and returned to my room with hair clippers, clothes, and two or three pairs of shoes for me to try on.

I received a call from Liberian vice president Joseph Boakai. Before connecting me with the vice president, his chief of staff said to me, "So tell me, what do the pearly gates look like?" We laughed. Vice President Boakai came on the line and congratulated me on my recovery, and I assured him that I would continue trying to help the people of his country overcome the outbreak.

Then I finished typing up my statement for my discharge press conference and wrote some e-mails.

Tim Viertel's wife, Jan, had joined him in Atlanta, and they brought Amber and me dinner from Cracker Barrel. The two of us sat beside each other on the bed and ate our first meal together off the little bedside table. We had turned off the main, fluorescent light in the room and ate with dimmed lighting.

After Amber left for the night, two of the nurses came into the room and did squats and push-ups with me.

∾

Word had begun to circulate among the hospital staff that I had been moved out of isolation and that a press conference was scheduled for Thursday morning. The doctors and nurses were going to stand behind Amber and me as I spoke, so the nurses knew they would be on television.

When the hospital staff started showing up in the morning, we noticed that they were wearing matching blue scrubs, some had gotten haircuts, and some were wearing more elaborate makeup than usual.

One of the guys said, "My wife plucked my eyebrows last night. She told me, 'You are going to be on national TV. You can't be having those bushy eyebrows.'"

We were able to get to know some great nurses while we were at Emory.

When I came out of my room to walk to the press conference, I was met by the high energy of the doctors, nurses, and lab technicians waiting for me in the hallway.

The doctors who had treated me were at the front of the line, and I embraced each one. I had planned on hugging every member of the team, but when I looked at how many were lined up down the hallway, I commented that it would take forever to get to each one of them.

"How about high-fives?" someone suggested.

So I went into a tunnel of nurses and techs with their hands extended, high-fiving me as I jogged through—finally touching the hands that had cared for me through two pairs of gloves for all those days.

MEETING THE MEDIA

Nancy's departure from the hospital had happened without the media knowing. When Dr. Ribner announced that I had been determined to be Ebola free and discharged, he also revealed that Nancy had left the hospital two days before.

In speaking about Nancy and me, Dr. Ribner said, "Their hope and faith have been an inspiration to all of us."

I was glad to hear such an affirming statement from my caregivers. They truly had been my friends and family for my three weeks of treatment in Atlanta. They had touched my life deeply, and I was glad that the sentiment was mutual. I had prayed that I would be faithful during my illness, but I never expected my faith to inspire my health-care team.

I stepped to the podium, with Amber to my right, took a deep breath, and looked down to my notes.

"Today is a miraculous day," I began. "I am thrilled to be alive, to be well, and to be reunited with my family."

I spoke for six-and-a-half minutes, providing for the media an overview of how we had entered the battle with Ebola in Liberia and about being struck with the disease. When I described being sick in bed in Monrovia as my condition had worsened each day, I said, "I prayed that God would help me be faithful even in my illness, and I prayed that in my life or in my death that he would be glorified. I did not know then, but have learned since, that there were thousands, maybe even millions, of people around the world praying for me throughout the week."

I had many people I wanted to thank, and I began with three groups: Samaritan's Purse, SIM Liberia, and the Emory hospital team that treated me. I thanked my family, my friends, my church family, and everyone who had been praying for me.

I expressed gratitude on Nancy's behalf, and I said that my family and I would be taking time to go away, out of the public eye, and reconnect.

"I am glad for any attention my sickness has attracted to the plight of West Africa in the midst of this epidemic," I concluded. "Please continue to pray for Liberia and the people of West Africa, and encourage those in positions of leadership and influence to do everything possible to bring this Ebola outbreak to an end. Thank you."

Amber and I then made good on our goal of embracing and thanking all the members of the medical team that had assembled behind us.

∽

We exited the hospital into a parking lot where Tim Viertel had a vehicle waiting for us. I took a deep breath of fresh air. I felt the ground beneath my feet and the sun's warmth on my face. Just four weeks earlier, I didn't know if I would ever have these experiences again. And now, hand in hand with Amber, I thanked God for life.

Some people might say God gave me a second chance, an opportunity to live better than I had up to this point. Others say there is nothing inherently redemptive about my situation and my narrow escape from death—it's just a matter of fact.

What I can say is this: I am alive and I am responsible for how I live today. I have never been more acutely aware of that truth than I was that afternoon, walking out of Emory Hospital, alive, well, and reunited with my wife.

PART 6

NEXT STEPS

18

Road to Recovery

Kent

After we left the hospital, Tim drove us to a smaller city outside of Atlanta for dinner at a LongHorn Steakhouse. Since this was our first venture out in public, we had no clue as to how I would be received.

To prevent being easily recognized following the televised news conference, I had changed into a different shirt, and Amber had handed me the only baseball cap she'd been able to find at a local drugstore: the red-and-white cap of the Druid Hills Red Devils high-school baseball team.

At the restaurant, where we were joined for dinner by a few representatives from Samaritan's Purse, I was wearing my Red Devils cap. Since I just did not feel right about wearing a cap at the table, though, I took it off and hung it on the back of my chair.

While we ate, one patron who was on his way out recognized me and headed toward our table. I wondered what he might say, but he graciously congratulated me on my recovery and thanked me for my work in Africa.

I had been out of the hospital maybe an hour, and already I could tell that our lives were going to be different.

∽

Going out in public made me nervous, because I could not anticipate how people would respond. It was a big unknown for us.

Amber and I planned to stay tucked away in a cabin in North Carolina, so the next day, before we left, we went to the grocery store to buy steak and chicken to grill. A little paranoid that I would be recognized, I put on my Red Devils cap, pulled it down low, and tried to avoid making eye contact with anyone.

We picked up our groceries, and I did not want to wait in line to check out. Standing still at the front of the store would have been asking to be identified. There were two Redbox machines not far from the cashier's stand, and I told Amber I would go see if there were any good movies to rent.

I was standing at one machine when a couple walked up to the one beside it. I turned at a bit of an angle, dropped my chin a little, and kept my eyes on the movie choices in front of me. Then I heard my name.

"Kent! Kent!"

It was Amber.

"I need a pen."

I looked over to Amber at the checkout stand, where she needed an ink pen to sign the receipt.

Are you kidding me?

The cashier tapped Amber on the shoulder and said, "Here, I have a pen."

The girl at the Redbox next to me discreetly motioned to the guy with her to look at me. I was so embarrassed. When we got in the car, I told Amber, "Please don't yell my name out in public."

We decided that from then on, anytime we needed to get each other's attention in public, she would call me Phil and I would call her Becky.

∽

Leaving the hospital, I felt good physically and even better mentally. I was ready to go—it didn't matter to where or for what, I wanted to do things. I had been discharged from Emory on a baby aspirin because my platelet count was a touch high, and I would be traveling a lot by car and airplane. I also was taking a stool softener for constipation and a steroid cream for psoriasis. Those were the only medications I needed to use.

Amber and I enjoy the outdoors, and we walked a nature trail the day of the grocery-store incident. We had ventured probably a half mile to the top of a hill, and I was running out of energy.

"We better stop and turn around," I told Amber. "If we walk down the other side of this hill, that means I will have to walk back up again."

We returned to the car, and that was my exercise for the day. I was done.

∾

The next day, August 23, was the day for our family reunion. Samaritan's Purse flew us to Indiana to pick up Ruby and Stephen. I had not seen them in a month, and they had been away from Amber for three weeks.

We landed at a small municipal airport, and when we walked down the steps, the kids came running across the tarmac. I got down on my knees and embraced both of them. It was a reunion of big, long, tight hugs.

"This is a really special day, right?" Ruby asked.

"Yes, it is," I told her.

The four of us plus my parents and my sister, Krista, ate at Cracker Barrel—which we had missed while living in Liberia—and returned to the airport for the trip back to North Carolina. We were so tired that all four of us slept the whole flight. I thought the fact that we could sleep peacefully was an indication of how good it was that we were back together.

We had set aside a period of family-only time in Asheville, North Carolina. The day after the round-trip flight to get the kids, I was wiped out and did little more than lounge on the couch and sleep. The next day, I felt up to taking a family walk, and by the time that was over, I was wiped out again.

That pattern of lacking energy and becoming fatigued after even minor activity continued over the next few weeks.

∽

On Tuesday, September 2, Matt Lauer of NBC spent most of the day interviewing us. Sitting and talking might not sound like it would take a lot of energy, but it was emotional for both Amber and me. This was the first time we had answered a lot of the questions about my illness—and the first time we heard each other talk about events from our own perspective. It was physically and mentally exhausting for me, but the heaviest emotional hit of the day came when I found out that Rick Sacra had Ebola.

After Nancy and I had become ill with Ebola in July, Rick had returned to Liberia to work in the hospital since primary health care was almost nonexistent in the midst of the outbreak. Now after a few intense weeks of working in the hospital, Rick had also been diagnosed with Ebola. John Fankhauser had called me from the airport just an hour before our interview with Matt Lauer to tell me about Rick's diagnosis. John was on his way back to Liberia to help take care of Rick and to do Rick's job in the hospital.

It was my initial meeting with Rick that had led to Amber and me choosing to go to Liberia. We had worked together only a couple of months before Rick and his family returned to the United States. He had come back to Liberia for three weeks the following February, and he also had returned to West Africa to work at the hospital while Dr. Debbie and I attended the CMDA conference in Greece. Rick and I were able to spend only a few days together then. Even though we had not spent as much time together in Liberia as we had hoped, nonetheless we had become close friends.

I learned that Rick would be traveling from Liberia to the Nebraska Medical Center in Omaha the next day. Later in the day on Thursday I received a call asking if I could fly to Omaha early Friday morning and donate plasma for Rick—he and I had the same blood type.

Without hesitation I said yes. I knew how critical a blood transfusion at the right time could be.

PLASMA FOR A COLLEAGUE

My transfusion from Gebah had been a whole-blood transfusion. Although we knew that a plasma transfusion would be preferable for fighting the virus, in all of sub-Saharan Africa, there was only one place with the capability to fractionate blood products (separate the plasma from the red blood cells), and that was in South Africa. Any transfusion in Liberia had to be whole blood.

Whole blood consists of red blood cells, white blood cells, and plasma. Plasma is the water part of the blood that contains all the proteins, including antibodies, which are what help our immune systems bind up viruses and bacteria in our blood. With help from ZMapp and supportive care, my body had mounted an immune response that was sufficient for me to survive. That meant my body had produced a large number of antibodies against Ebola.

If my plasma containing those antibodies could be given to Rick, just as the ZMapp had in theory done for me, my antibodies could bind up the virus in Rick's blood and not allow the virus to continue to replicate. That, in turn, would buy more time for his body to mount its own full immune response.

One advantage of taking only plasma from me was the body's ability to replace the plasma more quickly than it could red blood cells. Red blood cells typically require 100 to 120 days to be completely replenished. But if we drink plenty of water and stay hydrated, our bodies can replace plasma within twenty-four hours. That's why standard recommendations for giving blood are to wait at least eight weeks between donations, while plasma can be donated more frequently—sometimes up to three times in one week. That quick replenishing is not why I donated plasma instead of whole blood, but it did provide the benefit of allowing me to donate more frequently.

Amber was worried about my going to Nebraska. It wasn't that she did not want me to go, because we both would do anything we could to help Rick. But she was concerned that I might overexert myself on the trip, so her brother and dad accompanied me to Nebraska. The hospital had a wheelchair ready for me at all times during the few hours I was there, but I walked everywhere we went.

We flew back to North Carolina just in time to watch the interview with Matt Lauer on television. He had been great to us, both professional and courteous, so we were not disappointed with the program.

∾

On Monday, we drove to the international headquarters of Samaritan's Purse in Boone, where we met Franklin Graham and spent a couple of quality hours talking with him. We spoke at the staff devotional on Tuesday and took part in meetings all day on Wednesday. It was a long week for me.

On the drive back to Asheville, I started feeling really bad. By the time we arrived back to our cabin, I was nauseated, weak, fatigued, and dizzy. Everything was spinning around me. My parents had driven in on Monday to meet us at SP, and my dad, always the doctor, kept checking on me. I could not exert myself at all, and the only thing I felt like doing was lying on the couch.

That was easily the worst I had felt since leaving Emory, and it lasted for a few days.

During that time, I was preparing for a trip to Washington, DC, to testify to Congress about the Ebola epidemic. Melissa Strickland came to Asheville to work with me on my testimony on Friday and Saturday. On Monday, Amber and I flew to DC.

I was starting to feel okay the day of the flight, and we had a couple of very busy days scheduled in Washington.

I had been asked to testify to a House subcommittee on September 17. Ken Isaacs of Samaritan's Purse had testified at a hearing in early August, and this was the follow-up hearing.

Tim Viertel, the former Secret Service agent now working for SP, asked if we wanted to tour the White House while we were in DC. Of course we did! Then Tim told us that if President Obama was told our names were on the visitors' list for the tour, he would probably want to meet us.

Then I received an invitation to testify at a Senate subcommittee hearing scheduled for Tuesday, September 16, the day before the House hearing. The president announced that he would visit the CDC on Tuesday, and we assumed that would preclude our meeting him.

On Monday, we learned that the president's plans for the CDC visit had changed: he moved his trip to Atlanta to the afternoon, and we were invited to meet President Obama at the White House the next day.

I woke up Tuesday morning and read that the White House had released the president's plan of action for our country's response to Ebola. I'd had to submit my testimonies forty-eight hours in advance and had to make some last-minute adjustments because of the White House's announcement.

MEETING THE PRESIDENT

We met the president in a small office where we had been waiting for him. He came in and shook our hands.

"Let's step in here and take a picture," he said, motioning toward his office. *The Oval Office.*

We posed for a photo in front of his desk, and then he led us to a couch, where Amber and I sat while he took a seat in a chair next to us. We talked for five minutes or so, then stood for more posed pictures.

President Obama was very personable and nice.

To be honest, I had not thought meeting the president would be that big of a deal. I do not follow politics much. I do not dislike either Republicans or Democrats, but I am not a fan of politics.

Meeting President Obama, however, was an extraordinary experience.

While we were talking, I wanted to look around the Oval Office, but the leader of the free world was sitting five feet from me asking me questions. So instead of looking at everything, I maintained eye contact and said, "Yes sir, I feel good, thank you." We talked briefly about the plans for a US response in West Africa, and I tried to convey to the president the real sense of urgency that would be necessary to stop the epidemic.

Two White House staffers were with us in the Oval Office. One had not previously met the president. As we walked out of the office, out of earshot from the president, I said, "He wasn't as tall as I expected."

The staffer agreed.

GAINING STRENGTH

During our two days in DC, we met the president, I testified before congressional committees twice, and we walked around sightseeing. It was an exciting and energy-consuming two days.

Then we flew to Atlanta and spent the night there. I saw my doctors the next morning for my first post-Ebola checkup. Nancy and David also came to Atlanta, and we ate lunch together—the first time we had all been together since Nancy had left the hospital. After lunch the four of us attended a reception for all our health-care team members: doctors, nurses, lab techs, everybody. Amber and I spent that night in Atlanta and drove to Indiana the next day.

At the end of a very long, busy week, I realized that I did not feel terrible. That week was the beginning of my final phase of improvement. I still did not have as much energy as I wanted, and it took time to build up my stamina, but I felt good from then on and started regaining my energy.

Not long after this, Rick had recovered enough to be nearing his release from the Nebraska Medical Center. There had been a lot of survivors of Ebola in the world, but not many of them had been cared for quite the way Rick, Nancy, and I had been. Gebah was the only survivor I had known, but he had never been very sick. There just was not much research available on how Ebola survivors recovered.

I talked to Rick and suggested, based on my experience, that he take it easy at first, because his mind would probably tell him that his body was stronger than it truly was. I tried to pass that advice along to any Ebola survivor I talked with. I also donated plasma anytime I could for Ebola patients in the United States.

On September 28, Thomas Eric Duncan, a Liberian man in Dallas, Texas, became the first person to be diagnosed with Ebola in America. We were visiting family in Michigan when we heard the news. Amber and I were heartbroken to hear his story and followed updates on his condition very closely.

Several days later we were driving from Michigan to Kansas to visit friends when I received a phone call from Dr. Angela Hewlett in Nebraska. Ashoka Mukpo, a freelance cameraman working for NBC in Liberia, had contracted Ebola and had been evacuated to Nebraska, to the same unit where my friend Rick had been successfully treated. Angela said I had the same blood type as Ashoka and asked if I could donate plasma for him.

We went to a small blood bank in Kansas City that drew my plasma, which was then flown to Nebraska. After a short stay with friends in Kansas, we drove to Texas. Along the way we learned the tragic news of Mr. Duncan's death.

In Texas we attended Abilene Christian University's homecoming weekend, where Amber and I had opportunities to speak and we and the children were honored to serve as grand marshals for the homecoming parade.

That same weekend, I flew out to North Carolina to speak at the annual Prescription for Renewal conference that Samaritan's Purse holds for Christian physicians and dentists, and I was there when the story broke that a nurse in Dallas, Nina Pham, had contracted Ebola.

Dr. Aneesh Mehta from Emory called me on Sunday morning, October 12, saying that the CDC had called him that morning informing him that I had the same blood type as the nurse. He then asked if I would donate plasma for her.

I was scheduled to fly back to Abilene that day, but we arranged to stop in Dallas on the way. Staff members from Texas Health Presbyterian Hospital picked me up at the airport and drove me to their hospital, where I donated plasma for Nina Pham. I was able to meet her parents and a sister while I was donating, and we talked and prayed together for Nina.

The doctors asked if I would be willing to donate a second time for Nina. Amber and I had planned on returning to Fort Worth from Abilene on Wednesday, and we arranged for another plasma donation then.

On that Wednesday, it was announced that Amber Vinson, a nurse who worked at the same hospital, also had tested positive for Ebola. I was already scheduled to donate for Nina that day, but because she was in stable condition and Vinson's and my blood type matched, my plasma that day went to Amber instead.

I had found a new role in the fight against Ebola.

19

The Call Continues

Kent

There is a tension in the midst of crisis—a tension between fear and compassion. Much of the reaction to Ebola that we witnessed in the United States between August and November of 2014 was evidence of fear trumping compassion.

We saw public-health policy guided by fear rather than by the best available science. We saw some victims of Ebola—and even some healthy individuals who volunteered to fight against the virus—treated not like victims or heroes, but like criminals and dangerous public threats. These attitudes toward Ebola fighters and victims break my heart. Not just for the victims of this public approach, but for the public itself. When we discriminate against the very people on whom we ought to have compassion, we lose empathy, become callous, and erode our own humanity.

When Jesus was asked to name the greatest commandment, he replied, "Love the Lord your God with all your heart and with all your soul and with all your mind and with all your strength." It was also Jesus who said that you cannot love God if you do not love your neighbor. And our neighbor is not only the person who lives down the street from us. Our neighbor, Jesus says, is anyone whose path we cross, anyone who is in need.

When I think of the man who died in our unit from Ebola because he had helped carry a dead body from a taxi into a widow's home, I do not see him as a Liberian tragedy. I see him as Harris, my neighbor, who died trying to do good for others.

Jesus taught us to love our neighbors as ourselves. We live in a global community, and we must recognize our neighbors in this community. And we must not allow fear to overcome our sense of compassion for our neighbors who are in need.

GOD DID SAVE MY LIFE

During my news conference at Emory, I credited God for my survival, saying,

> I cannot thank you enough for your prayers and your support. But what I can tell you is that I serve a faithful God who answers prayers. Through the care of the Samaritan's Purse and SIM missionary team in Liberia, the use of an experimental drug, and the expertise and resources of the health care team at Emory University Hospital, God saved my life—a direct answer to thousands and thousands of prayers. I am incredibly thankful to all of those who were involved in my care, from the first day of my illness all the way up until today, the day of my release from Emory.

I know that some considered it controversial for me to claim that God saved my life when I had received an experimental drug and some of the greatest medical care available in the world. I can see how those two realities appear to contradict each other. I also feel the dissonance with claiming that God saved my life while thousands of others died.

These issues are not clear-cut for me. I wrestle with these tensions. I cannot explain how I was healed. Was there a supernatural intervention that reversed the course of my illness? Or was the miracle in the fact that a new, untested treatment for a rare disease had been produced in a greenhouse in Kentucky, and a single course of that drug found its way to my bedside in Liberia on the day that I was about to die? Or did the miracle lie in the fact that I was born in the United States, and the Department of State leveraged all the resources at its disposal to bring me back home to one of the world's premier medical centers for treatment? Or perhaps the miracle was in the preparation of the Airborne Biomedical Containment Systems by CDC and Phoenix Air six years before Ebola ever surfaced in West Africa? Or could it be that the miracle was in John Fankhauser's insight to give me supplemental potassium, despite a paucity of data to suggest such an intervention in the face of Ebola?

So many pieces of the puzzle came together in just the right way at just the right time to provide me with the care that saved my life. Some may call it all a grand coincidence, and I couldn't argue against them. But when I see the unlikely and highly improbable events that occurred—not only during my illness, but also for decades preceding the Ebola epidemic in West Africa—I see the hand of God at work, and I give him the credit.

∾

In November of 2014, I had the privilege of visiting Kentucky BioProcessing (KBP) where ZMapp was produced. The drug was the result of the combined work of a small San Diego company, Mapp Biopharmaceutical; USAMRIID; the United States National Institutes of Health; and the Public Health Agency of Canada.

The scientists of those institutions agreed to collaborate on their work in an industry that is typically defined by competition. Scientists advance in their field by making the next big discovery. But these scientists set aside potential personal glory in an effort to seek the good of humanity. They shared their discoveries and combined their developed treatments into a synergistic cocktail more effective than anything either institution had been able to produce on its own.

Their work, built on the shoulders of seven Nobel prizes in science, was placed in the hands of KBP, a small company seeking to establish a place for tobacco in the world of biopharmaceutical protein production. The company's CEO, Hugh Haydon, explained to us KBP's unlikely history.

For nearly two decades, the use of tobacco to produce biopharmaceutical proteins had struggled to gain acceptance. While other companies working in this area had come and gone, KBP managed to survive with a collaborative approach, focusing on products that others had little interest in and on creating a market for its services. Its leaders dreamed of using their proprietary technique of producing pharmaceutical proteins in tobacco plants to revolutionize the industry.

KBP started by growing its own tobacco seed, but had to develop a process for making the tiny, heterogeneous seeds uniform so that they could be picked up by a machine and planted one seed at a time into black plastic trays. Trays had to be engineered that could be managed by the robot used in one step of the process. The manager of the agricultural department produced and stored a quantity of seed that, at the rate of usage then, would have been enough for thirty years.

When someone inside the company asked why so much seed needed to be produced, no one had a good answer. The company proceeded anyway. Over and over, KBP's leadership made business decisions that did not appear to make good short-term business sense but reflected a long-term faith in their objectives.

Then a project came in asking the company to make a small amount of three different proteins to be tested in monkeys as a treatment for Ebola Virus Disease. KBP made enough of the final product for the animal trials, with just a little extra to spare. It was a small amount of that product that ended up at my bedside in Liberia on July 31, 2014. And because of KBP's preparation, when asked to ramp up its production of ZMapp in the face of the worsening outbreak, the company was positioned to do so, down to the last detail—even the amount of seed needed for the expanded production.

A scientist from NIH was present at KBP on the day of our tour. After he listened to the company history and then gave the input of his role in developing one of the antibodies used in ZMapp, he came to this conclusion: The miracles of God do not have to be momentary supernatural occurrences. The miracles of God can be seen in details over decades.

∾

Honestly, I wrestle with the theology of my recovery sometimes. I am convinced that there is nothing special about me that would persuade God to save my life while others were dying. I will never claim that my faith must have been in some way superior to the faith of the masses that died in West Africa. I do not believe that the survival of one person and the death of another indicates anything about the worth or faithfulness or merit of either person. I also have a hard time believing, as many might say, that God had every detail of this experience planned out ahead of time.

I do not claim to know how God works. But this I do know: I was facing death, and now I am alive. And with life comes responsibility. Saint Paul put it this way: "For to me, to live is Christ and to die is gain."[16] I might put it this way: Because I live, I ought to use my life in a way that is meaningful and helpful to my neighbor. This is not for my own glory; it is for God, who gave me life.

CALLED FOR LIFE

I once hoped that after a long career as a missionary, I would have an experience worth writing about that might inspire someone in my shoes forty years behind me. I never anticipated anything like our current circumstances.

Amber and I went to Liberia as anonymous, quiet missionaries wanting to live meaningful lives. Our family's mind-set moving there resonated with Psalm 105:1–3:

> Give thanks to the LORD, call on his name;
>> make known among the nations what he has done.
> Sing to him, sing praise to him;
>> tell of all his wonderful acts.
> Glory in his holy name;
>> let the hearts of those who seek the LORD rejoice.

Our goal was simple. We prayed, *God, we want to tell people about you. We want to serve people in a way that will bring them to know you.*

Some days I feel like God has responded, *Oh, you want to tell people about me, huh? Here, try this platform. Here is a press conference with eighteen million viewers. Here, testify to world leaders.*

In one sense our calling all along was to make God's name known. In another sense we moved to West Africa to serve the people of Liberia, to do good for them, and to help improve their lives. In my mind these two goals are inseparable. To do one without the other is to leave the job unfinished.

This new platform, while obviously providing us with a louder voice, in a very real way may also allow us to help Liberia on a much larger scale, impacting tens of thousands. With this larger platform we have been given, we encourage people to pray for Liberians and to partner with them as they rebuild their country and their health-care system.

Post-Ebola, Amber and I feel like our family is in a new season of life. Seasons come and go. This season has come, and we expect that it will eventually go. We might become medical missionaries again—we might return to what we knew as our calling before all this happened. Deep in the core of my heart, I still feel like this is who we are and what we were made to do.

∾

We frequently are asked if we will return to Liberia.

We simply do not know.

One thing we do know, though, is that we won't ever be able to return to the same Liberia, because Liberia will never again be the same place we moved to in 2013.

War changed the country before we got there, and the war against Ebola has changed it once again. The civil wars left scars on the people—their bodies as well as their minds. Those who survived the wars told us that Ebola was another war for their country to fight. Except this enemy, a microscopic virus, was unseen, and that made it more frightening.

The most updated figures as of this writing cite more than twenty-six thousand reported cases of Ebola in Guinea, Liberia, and Sierra Leone, with more than eleven thousand deaths. That is more than seven times the number of Ebola deaths worldwide in all previous outbreaks combined. The number of deaths in Liberia has exceeded four thousand.

Liberians are an affectionate people who love to shake hands in greeting. A finger-snap handshake was the common way of greeting when we were there. Two people would slap hands, slide their fingers down each other's palms, and end the handshake with a mutual finger snap.

Because of Ebola, Liberians stopped touching each other. Maybe after the threat has been extinguished, they will resume their unique handshake. But the country and the people have been scarred, just as they were by the civil wars. Although the Ebola crisis is still not over, our spirits already ache at the thought of Liberia having to recover from another battle.

Even if we end up back at ELWA with Samaritan's Purse, that will never be the same either. The same group of people will not be there, we won't have the same neighbors as before, and we might not live in the same house. Their children and our children will have grown up apart from each other for an important period of their lives.

There are very few people who lived through the crisis with us and can understand how life is different because of it. And now those few people are scattered all over the globe. The loss of that community saddens me.

∾

I have been asked frequently how I, personally, have changed as a result of contracting Ebola.

As far as recovering from the disease, I believe I was back to 100 percent by

Christmas 2014, four months after leaving the hospital. I am thankful that I do not have any negative physical aftereffects.

ZMapp was an experimental drug when I received it. Only time will tell if there are any long-term effects that were previously unknown.

But I am alive. Any concerns that could develop down the road will be viewed through that lens.

I cannot answer yet how my experience will change my practice as a doctor. But it has impacted me greatly. Being the recipients of such grace and generosity as we have been is humbling. I think that humility is a measure of the impact, but that does not indicate its full effect going forward. My hope, my prayer, is that I will become a more compassionate husband, a more compassionate father, a more compassionate physician, and a more compassionate neighbor.

When I knelt next to Felicia on that rainy June night outside our hospital, I told myself that everything was about to change. I had no idea how true that was. But one thing has not changed: our desire to live faithful to God's calling.

Our calling is to be faithful wherever we are, to be good stewards of opportunities, to be responsible with what we have been given, to try to do good, and to serve those whose paths we cross.

For to me, to live is Christ and to die is gain.

Epilogue

Gratitude

Kent

My family has a tradition of gathering at my parents' home every other year for Christmas. With our move to Liberia, we assumed that we would not be able to be there in 2014. My sickness changed that.

Amber, the kids, and I spent a little more than a week in Indianapolis at my parents' home for the holiday. By this time, I was beginning to feel like I had fully recovered.

One of the first items on our to-do list was visit the apple orchard where I had taken Amber the first time she came to Indianapolis for the Broncos-Colts game. The orchard also was one of the last places we visited on our final trip to see my parents before moving to Liberia. That trip came during the fall, after most of the apples had been harvested and as the pumpkins were almost ripe. We took our family picture there sitting on a bench.

The four of us returned to that orchard during our Christmas trip, enjoyed their tasty apple-cider slushes, and posed for an updated family picture.

My three brothers and two sisters are scattered across the country: Michigan, Georgia, Texas, and Indiana. We were able to all be together for about three days. There were twenty-four of us at my mom and dad's, including nieces and nephews, plus the five dogs my brother Kevin, a veterinarian, brought with his family all the way from Georgia.

The grandkids played in the basement, where my mom has kept the toys that survived the six of us. We shared one of my favorite meals—biscuits and gravy, scrambled eggs and bacon, and lots of coffee. To keep my strength up (and negate that meal), I did a boot-camp workout with my three teenage nieces.

My dad was proud that our schedules had worked out so that we all were able to attend church together, which we had not done in several years. When he gave the welcome from the podium, he pointed out that all his family was with him that morning, including the newest member of the clan, eleven-month-old Sydney.

The trip was a wonderful time of simply being together as a family.

We had all agreed in advance not to exchange presents. We did not want to give and receive gifts, but instead spend our time focusing on the gift that we had all received: being together again.

∾

On Sunday evening, December 28, the entire family was gathered in the dining room, and I took advantage of having everyone assembled to say something I had not planned.

Since being cleared of Ebola, I have had the opportunity to thank many people in person who played a role in my recovery. I have been able to talk with and thank all the doctors and the team that cared for me at Emory. I have met President Obama, the president of Phoenix Air, and the nurse who accompanied me on my flight from Liberia to Atlanta. I've expressed my appreciation to officials with Health and Human Services, the CDC, the NIH, and the FDA. I have spoken to large groups of people who had prayed for me, and I have thanked them.

But that evening at the dining-room table, I had an opportunity to thank all my family members at the same time. Too often, we forget to thank the people who are closest to us. They are easy to take for granted, and we can expend all our patience and niceties on strangers and have only leftovers to give our family.

My family had prayed earnestly for me, they had taken care of Amber like she was their daughter or sister, they had acted as parents to Ruby and Stephen, and they had traveled to the hospital to visit me. During a nerve-racking time of fear and uncertainty for them, they had represented our family well, both with the caretakers at Emory and with the media. Even before then, they had supported Amber and me, without reservation, when we announced we were moving to Africa.

So for a few minutes, I thanked the people who mean the most to me.

As I spoke from my heart and looked into the attentive faces around my parents' dining room, I could clearly sense that we all shared a deep emotion of gratitude to God. It was more than just gratitude for the outcome, that I was alive. We shared a sense of gratitude for how God had lovingly carried our family through our trial.

He had given us everything we needed to be faithful to him.

Acknowledgments

We first want to thank all the Ebola fighters with Samaritan's Purse; ELWA Hospital; SIM; Liberian, Sierra Leonean, and Guinean Ministries of Health; World Health Organization; Médecins Sans Frontières; Centers for Disease Control and Prevention; US Public Health Service; National Institutes of Health; USAID; UNICEF; USAMRIID; Partners in Health; International Medical Corps; Save the Children; and so many more who have gone to West Africa to help during this Ebola outbreak. You are heroes.

We offer sincere gratitude to our parents, Mama and Daddy (Dr. Jim and Jan Brantly) and Daddy and Mom (Donnie and Lisa Carroll) for the gift of life; Dr. Kerry and Shelley Brantly for keeping our kids safe, happy, well fed, and teeth brushed; Krista Brantly for your consistent presence and your help with this book; and all the rest of our siblings and their spouses for your understanding, help, loyalty, company, prayers, and support.

We thank Samaritan's Purse, Franklin Graham, Ken Isaacs, Dr. Richard Furman, Ed Morrow, Melissa Strickland, Mary Elizabeth Jameson, Dr. Lance Plyler, Tim and Jan Viertel, Dr. Linda Mobula, John Freyler, Dr. Tom Wood, Dr. Nathalie MacDermott, Dr. Ed Carns, Allison Rolston, Kathy Mazzella, Kelly Sites, Tim Mosher, Wil Graham, Eric Wilkes, the Billy Graham Training Center at the Cove, and Mark DeMoss.

To our dear friends and coworkers at ELWA: David and Nancy Writebol, the Fankhauser family, the Buller family, the Neiss family, the Sacra family, the Kauffeldt family, Joni Byker, the Simpson family, Dr. Debbie, the Wendyue family, and the many other SP and SIM missionaries and Christian workers who "did life" with us. We love you and miss you.

For their part in Kent's evacuation and treatment, we thank the president of the United States of America, the Honorable Barack Obama; Dr. William Walters, director of operational medicine at the State Department; secretary of Health and Human Services, the Honorable Sylvia Mathews Burwell; and Melissa Rogers, special assistant to the president and executive director of the White House Office of Faith-Based and Neighborhood Partnerships.

For welcoming the first patient with Ebola to be treated on US soil, we thank Emory University Hospital, Dr. Bruce Ribner, Dr. Colleen Kraft, Dr. G. Marshall Lyon III, Dr. Aneesh Mehta, Dr. Jay Varkey, Robert J. Bachman, Susan M. Grant, Sean Kaufman, and the incredible team of nurses, medical assistants, lab technicians, paramedics, dieticians, custodians, and security officers.

Thanks to all our friends at Southside Church of Christ and John Peter Smith Hospital in Fort Worth, Texas; Dr. Steve and Lindsay Cloer; Randy Harris; Scott and Tricia Parker; Dr. David and Joan McRay; Alan and Jan Hegi; Dr. Jason and Italia Brewington; and Kent and Joan Smith.

For their commendable hospitality, we thank Dr. Jack and Ann Griggs, Jami Amerine, Dr. Tim and Angie Martin, and Dr. Gary and Frances Green.

For saying yes when asked to do something extraordinary, we thank Phoenix Air Group Inc., Dent Thompson, Dr. Doug Olson, Vance Ferebee, Jonathan Jackson, and the flight crew.

For their years of research, ingenuity, collaboration, and perseverance, we thank Kentucky BioProcessing Inc., Mapp Biopharmaceutical, Larry Zeitlin, Hugh Haydon, Dr. Gary Kobinger of the National Microbiology Laboratory of Canada, Dr. Lisa Hensley of NIH, and Dr. Gene Olinger of NIH.

For their generosity, we thank the Layne family; the Williams family; the JPS Foundation; the Liberian Association of North Texas; Mrs. Joyce Brown; Mrs. Elizabeth Tubman; Roy Charles Brooks; Tarrant county commissioner, precinct 1; Southern Hills Church of Christ; Southeastern Church of Christ; Tim Cook; Michael Pothoff; Michael Hall; and the hundreds of others who sent cards, gifts, and household items.

We would like to thank the people who made this book possible: our gumptious agent, Chris Park, Foundry Literary and Media; our enduring writer, David Thomas; the remarkable team at Crown / WaterBrook Multnomah, including our supportive advocate in New York, Tina Constable; our hopeful publisher, Alexander Field; our diligent editor, Bruce Nygren; and Melanie Larson, for your encouragement, advice, and expertise.

Last on this list, but by no means least, to the many people who prayed, fasted, and meditated, we give our sincerest and most heartfelt thanks.

Notes

1. 2 Timothy 1:7, NLT.
2. "Today O," lyrics by Wale Adenuga, copyright 1997, *Fountain of Praise/ACSAP.* Used by permission.
3. Mark 6:34.
4. Mark 12:28–31.
5. Hebrews 3:15.
6. See Hebrews 4:11.
7. Hebrews 4:16.
8. Philippians 3:10–11.
9. Philippians 1:21.
10. "Be with Me, Lord," music by L. O. Sanderson, lyrics by T. O. Chisholm, copyright 1934, public domain.
11. "Great Is Thy Faithfulness," music by W. M. Runyan, lyrics by T. O. Chisholm, copyright 1923, renewed 1951, Hope Publishing Company.
12. "I Need Thee Every Hour," music by Jars of Clay, *Redemption Songs,* copyright 2005; lyrics by Annie Sherwood Hawks, copyright 1872.
13. C. S. Lewis, *The Lion, the Witch and the Wardrobe* (New York: MacMillan, 1970), 75–76.
14. John 16:33, NLT.
15. See Daniel 3.
16. Philippians 1:21.

List of Abbreviations

ABCS—Airborne Biomedical Containment Systems

ACU—Abilene Christian University in Texas

AIDS—see HIV below

CDC—Centers for Disease Control and Prevention, in the United States

CMDA—Christian Medical and Dental Associations

DKA—diabetic ketoacidosis

ELWA—Eternal Love Winning Africa, SIM's mission in Liberia, founded
in 1952

ELWA Hospital—Eternal Love Winning Africa Hospital, Paynesville,
Monrovia, Liberia

ELWA 1—hospital chapel converted to ETU

ELWA 2—the second, larger ETU

ETU—Ebola Treatment Unit, a.k.a. isolation unit

EVD—Ebola Virus Disease

GI—gastrointestinal

HIV—human immunodeficiency virus, a lentivirus that causes the acquired
immunodeficiency syndrome (AIDS)

ICU—intensive care unit

JFK—John F. Kennedy Medical Center in Monrovia, Liberia

JPS—John Peter Smith Hospital in Fort Worth, Texas

KBP—Kentucky BioProcessing

MSF—Médecins Sans Frontières, commonly referred to as Doctors Without
Borders

NIAID—National Institute of Allergy and Infectious Disease, in the United
States

NIH—National Institutes of Health, in the United States

OB—obstetrics

ORS—oral rehydration solution

PPE—personal protective equipment

RDT—rapid diagnostic test for malaria

SARS—severe acute respiratory syndrome, a viral respiratory disease

SCDU—Serious Communicable Diseases Unit

SIM—Serving In Mission, a Christian mission organization

SP—Samaritan's Purse International Relief

UNICEF—United Nations Children's Fund

UNMIL—United Nations Mission in Liberia

USAMRIID—US Army Medical Research Institute of Infectious Diseases

WHO—World Health Organization

About the Authors

Dr. Kent and Amber Brantly served as medical missionaries with Samaritan's Purse in Monrovia, Liberia, from October 2013 to August 2014. Kent was the medical director for the only Ebola treatment unit in all of southern Liberia when he was diagnosed with Ebola Virus Disease. He became the first person with Ebola to be treated in the United States when he was evacuated to Emory University Hospital.

Kent received his medical degree from Indiana University School of Medicine and completed his family medicine residency and his fellowship in maternal child health at John Peter Smith Hospital in Fort Worth, Texas. He also holds a bachelor of arts in biblical text from Abilene Christian University in Abilene, Texas. Amber earned a bachelor of science in nursing, also from Abilene Christian University, and she worked as a surgical nurse before becoming a mother.

The Brantlys feel it is their privilege and duty to speak out on behalf of the people of West Africa who continue to suffer from the scourge of Ebola. They currently live with their two young children, Ruby and Stephen, in Fort Worth, where Kent is serving as medical missions advisor for Samaritan's Purse.